WHAT TEACHERS DO

Philip Garner, Viv Hinchcliffe and Sarah Sandow are all members of staff at the School of Education, Brunel University (formerly the Education Department of the West London Institute). They have worked closely together in the provision of Diploma and Master's courses for teachers and in writing about special education over the past eight years. Philip Garner has worked in secondary schools and in units for children with behavioural difficulties. Viv Hinchcliffe was formerly a teacher of children with severe learning difficulties, and Sarah Sandow worked in a hospital school as a peripatetic support teacher for such children and their parents before entering the wider special eduction field. Since 1987 they have together worked with several hundred teachers in ordinary and special schools.

WHAT TEACHERS DO:

DEVELOPMENTS IN SPECIAL EDUCATION

Philip Garner
Viv Hinchcliffe
and
Sarah Sandow

P·C·P
Paul Chapman
Publishing Ltd

Paul Chapman Publishing Ltd
144 Liverpool Road
London
N1 1LA

British Library Cataloguing in Publication Data
Garner, Philip
What Teachers Do: Developments in Special
Education
I. Title
371.9043
ISBN 1–85396–285–6

Typeset by Whitelaw & Palmer Ltd, Glasgow
Printed and bound by The Baskerville Press, Salisbury

A B C D E F G H   9 8 7 6 5

Contents

Preface

Special education has developed fully as a specialism within education during the past twenty years. That development has been accompanied by a flood of official publications, academic writing and practical advice for teachers. In-service education for teachers of children with special needs at first burgeoned, but later was subordinated to the demands of the 1988 Education Act. Funds for long courses, formerly advanced by Local Education Authorities, dried up, and school-based INSET attempted to fill the gap. Inevitably such short courses were forced to concentrate on instrumental issues and seldom allowed the teachers to engage in serious reflection. Nevertheless, a determined band of committed teachers have continued to advance their own and their pupils' progress through attending long courses at universities and colleges. The reflection which could not surface in short courses has been evident in the writing done by these teachers as part of their professional study. The authentic voice of the teacher in the classroom (and in the staffroom) should be heard by those who seek to join them, those who manage them and by those who criticise them.

This book is a celebration of the work of these teachers. It contains a representative sample of teachers' writing about their jobs, their ideas, their pupils and their customers which was first written in response to the requirements of the Diploma in Professional Studies in Education (Special Educational Needs) (DPSE SEN), the DPSE (Severe Learning Difficulties) or the MEd (SEN or SLD), courses held at the former West London Institute of Higher Education, now the School of Education, Brunel University. It demonstrates the range, complexity and quality of the work which teachers in special education do, whether they work in ordinary or in special schools, or sometimes take up advisory or peripatetic roles.

In collecting and arranging this work, we have tried to focus on the main areas of teacher activity. However, sometimes, where a piece of writing has demonstrated curriculum planning, management, negotiation *and* reflection, we have found it difficult to classify the extracts. We hope, nevertheless, that the reader will find excitement, coherence, and enlightenment in what we have selected.

In order to protect the schools, the children and the teachers themselves, we have not attached names to the extracts, and the initials which are used as identifiers do not bear any relation to the actual names of teachers or children. We are, however, glad to be able to thank the following teachers for permission to use their work.

Paul Adair, Sarah Andrews, Joe Apicella, Gill Atkin, Pauline Atkins, Ravinder Bakshi, Kathy Bale, Chandip Behar, Dianne Bennett, Jacqui Bertrand, Gary Boatman, Sheila Breckenridge, Mary Burke, Jenny Catcheside, Sandra Chambers, Daphne Coward, Helen Frith, Vivienne Greenwood, Rena Harris-Cooksley, Cathy Herries, Richard Hickson, Barbara Holloway, Gillian Hosler, Lorna Jaffa, Stella Johnston, Ian Jones, Di Kaufman, Mary Kelly, Odilia Kirst, Karen Lewis, Margaret Llewellyn, Chris Marris, Maureen Mitchell, Sally Mitchell, Ruth Muller, Christine Pepper, John Prior, Sister Julie Rose, Susan Shocket, Greg Simons, Jill Smyth, Jane Staves, Penny Stephen, Stephanie Theodolides, Donna Thomas, Margaret Upstill, Christine Wassell, Dave Waterman, Pat Watts, Bryony Williamson, Sandy Wilson, Lynn Young.

Philip Garner, Viv Hinchcliffe and Sarah Sandow

Introduction:
A Context for what Teachers Do

The way in which teachers do their jobs has been the focus of considerable recent attention (MacLure, 1993). It is no surprise that this growth in interest has occurred at a critical time for the profession as a whole, characterised by changed working practices, burgeoning legislative requirements and reductions in funding. The changes resulting from the 1988 Education Act have gathered increasing pace during the 1990s, and there is not a single aspect of the education system that has not been scrutinised, followed by 'the introduction of a plethora of policies and innovations covering all aspects of educational provision and practice' (Vlachou and Barton, 1994).

Not least amongst the targets for government attack was the in-service training and professional development (INSET) of teachers. In the post-ERA climate, when compulsory education was reorientating along instrumental, market-governed lines, a widely held view was that 'present patterns of training help to perpetuate a damagingly 'progressive' educational establishment, and so contribute significantly to low standards in the schools' (Edwards, 1992).

This scrutiny has been underpinned by an apparent wish, on the part of central government, to reduce teacher autonomy and power. This is particularly apparent with respect to the taught curriculum, which has become the property of successive Conservative governments; hitherto, apart from the ongoing debate concerning such matters as vocational preparedness of school-leavers and the apparent decline in standards of literacy and numeracy, teachers in classrooms were largely left to get on with their jobs.

In the period after 1988, control and criticism of teachers were combined. Legislation was introduced to govern their training and work-practices, and it occurred alongside a systematic, orchestrated criticism of the profession, in which 'teachers' voices have been largely neglected, their opinions overridden, and their concerns dismissed' (Hargreaves, 1990). In other words, teachers were not to be allowed the scope to think about what they do, for fear of subverting the political intent of post–1988 educational innovations.

Recent years have been littered with directives from central government concerning a vast range of educational matters. Most of these have to be absorbed, and acted upon, by teachers. The DfE (and formerly the DES) has vigorously supported government ideology in its associated written matter. This is presented, benignly, as 'guidance', or, in a more combative manner, as 'orders'. Teachers, whilst meeting the present needs of their pupils, have to digest a weekly diet of new instructions. For those working in the area of SEN this means consideration of both general education issues and that which is specifically focused on special needs. Teachers have consequently been faced with implementing a range of additional government initiatives (the Children Act, the 'Pupils with Problems' circulars and notably the SEN Code of Practice stand out as examples). They have also had to contend with the inference that SEN work carries less professional status than, for example, generic subject-based work. Those involved in SEN work in schools, being associated with the special needs of the children they teach, have been regarded by many as not 'proper teachers': the SEN support teacher is a case in point.

This chapter outlines a range of matters, relating both to general education and to SEN practice, which function as a backdrop to the work that teachers do with children who have learning difficulties. These are the concerns which SEN teachers always seem to return to, whether during INSET sessions or informal staffroom discussion. In doing this we will map the context for professional practice in SEN, against which a teacher's work is done, using a set of themes which, because of the complex nature of SEN, could easily be replaced by a parallel set of concerns. These themes do not comprise a comprehensive treatment of the factors which might inhibit SEN developments in the 1990s. Mittler (1992) contains a fuller account. What will immediately be apparent from their analysis is that financial, social and political concerns are as important as the legislative and procedural issues relating to assessment, identification and curriculum provision. Hopefully the present chapter serves to illustrate something of the practical and ideological dilemmas facing teachers who work in SEN. These will surface at various points in the accounts provided for this book.

INITIAL TEACHER EDUCATION AND INSET

Since the Education Reform Act (ERA) in 1988 teacher education as a whole (whether pre- or in-service) has undergone significant change. As with other areas of education it has become the focus of radical reform, based upon the view of central government that the training of teachers as a whole was dominated by left-wing anti-establishment liberals. A later chapter considers the implications of this state of affairs, and its impact on the wider professional development opportunities offered to serving teachers. For the present discussion it is sufficient to reaffirm that the late 1980s saw teacher education 'transformed from that quiet backwater into a major site for ideological struggle between the government and other groups with an interest in education' (Furlong, 1992). Two aspects of recent developments are noteworthy. They have a symbiotic relationship, in which what happens to students undertaking initial teacher training (ITT) courses has a critical effect on subsequent INSET and professional development opportunities. Both are considered in our final chapter.

At this stage, therefore, we want merely to note that the 'major site for ideological struggle' at the ITT stage, is characterised by a move towards school-based, rather than college-based, provision and by a commensurate reduction in the time devoted to SEN matters during courses of teacher training. Furthermore, the current situation is marked by a heavy emphasis upon skills and competences, at the expense of reflection.

The importance of these developments to serving teachers is that they impact upon every aspect of their working lives in succeeding years. Those involved in SEN work have to deal with a steadily increasing number of colleagues who have received no direct SEN input at ITT level. Nor will most new teachers have had the opportunity to explore the wider political, social and ethical questions raised by the way in which we currently provide for SEN. In this context, lack of information or awareness is likely to breed misunderstanding and prejudice.

INSET activity in SEN in England has also undergone a period of dramatic change in the last fifteen years. This reorientation can be linked to two things: changes in ideology, underpinned by legislation, and changes in the political economy of the country, both of which have meant that the further professional development of teachers in this aspect of education has assumed a pragmatic nature.

The 1981 Education Act drew to a close a period of intense debate about the segregation of those children in schools who had SEN. Importantly the Act made specific mention of the need to integrate such children into mainstream or normative educational environments. Moreover, in suggesting this shift in approach, the Act stated unequivocally that the old categories of handicap were to be replaced by a series of specifications which focused upon the learning needs of children.

Both elements of the Act are axiomatic: you cannot really have successful integration into mainstream schools without an attendant shift away from a 'within child' approach to handicap. In the latter the child remains an object of pity, derision, fear and scorn because, explicitly at times, and almost always implicitly, there is a belief that the child, or his/her family, have done something to cause the 'condition' in the first place. It is not, so the story goes, the responsibility of others to deal with the consequences.

The effects of the 1981 Education Act have been particularly felt in INSET. In the years following the Act there was a gradual increase in the integration of those children who were officially categorised as having a SEN (so that they were provided with a legally binding *statement* of what those needs were and how they were going to be met); Government thinking was that there should therefore be a concentration of the training effort upon those courses which prepared teachers for work with such children in mainstream schools (i.e.

generic undergraduate training courses for primary- and secondary-school specialists). SEN was to be developed as a 'permeated' topic within such courses of study, whilst specialist courses were to become an integral part of in-service provision.

As we have already noted, there are now no undergraduate courses leading to specialist teaching qualifications for those who wish to work solely with formally statemented children. This is justified in part by the gradual decrease in the numbers of children attending special schools, but also by the belief that in order to work with children who are developmentally delayed, socially malfunctioning, or organically disabled, a teacher must have some background in, and experience of, normal child development.

INSET in SEN has, usually, been provided in a number of ways. Those teachers who already possess a teaching qualification and some classroom experience can pursue courses of professional study leading towards a diploma or a master's degree in SEN, validated by a university or college. These in-service qualifications can either be very specifically orientated to a particular need (autistic, hearing impaired, or profound and multiply disabled children, for example) or be of a more general nature.

Local Education Authorities (LEAs) have been providers of INSET for a long time. With the advent of local management (LMS) they have had to amend the way in which they operated. Hitherto they had faced very little competition from independent providers and were secure in the knowledge that, notwithstanding the controls of the exchequer, they had a set sum of money to work with. They were therefore in a position to prioritise for SEN and planned accordingly, dependent upon the perceived INSET needs across the LEA. After 1988, however, the schools became the budget holders, and were therefore in a position to dictate who should attend what courses. The pressures placed on schools to implement a range of changes after 1988 have meant that SEN has had to compete with a host of other, often worthy, focuses for INSET. Moreover, the fragmentation of LEA-wide provision has led to the charge that much school-based INSET is parochial and narrow.

In both cases it is the day-release of teachers for attendance on courses which is expensive. Few LEAs and schools are able to allocate funds for supply-cover, and many are finding that increases in course fees have become prohibitive. As a result most practising teachers now attend part-time courses of study, particularly in the evenings. Moreover, with further action on the part of central government in reducing the financial power of those LEAs which traditionally have had high concentrations of children with special needs, teachers are increasingly having to pay for their own in-service courses. It should also be noted that those teachers who live and work some distance away from training institutions find it very difficult to participate in evening courses.

Against this background it is worth noting that Morant (1981) has argued that there are at least four types of professional need relating to INSET. In the first instance new teachers require *induction* training; more experienced teachers need what is termed *extension* training, providing them with broader professional interests and the basis for promotion. Thirdly, Morant notes the *refreshment* needs of teachers, applicable to those who are either returning to teaching or beginning a period of teaching a new specialism. Lastly, the *conversion* needs are identified, whereby new skills are provided to those teachers whose job specification is changed. To these we would add a fifth group: the *status* needs of teachers, a rationale for engaging in INSET activity which has been noted by Mittler (1993).

The INSET situation in England, therefore, is at once progressive and reactionary. On the one hand vigorous moves towards integration in the 1970s led to hopes that SEN issues would become fundamental to the training needs of all teachers. Regrettably, however, the rhetoric of education for the disabled does not take into account the provision of adequate funds to ensure the in-service training of those who teach them. Ideology and politico-economic commitment need to go hand in hand to ensure success.

GUIDANCE OR ORDER: YOU PAYS YOUR MONEY, YOU TAKES YOUR CODE

The Code of Practice on the Identification and Assessment of Special Educational Needs (DfE, 1994) is the most important SEN policy document of the 1990s. It can be divided into three main areas: policy, roles and procedures and practice. It should be noted that the Code is a non-statutory document, but that the regulations to which it frequently refers are statutory. The tension, between 'guidance' and 'statutory regulations', in this and other government documents is a matter to which many teachers make reference.

In common with legislation in special education dating from 1981, the Code of Practice contains substantial ambiguities, either by accident or design. Most notable amongst these is that schools are left to interpret the Code based upon 'the size, organisation, location and pupil population of the school' (p. ii). Further opportunity for misinterpretation (or manoeuvre) is apparent in the Code's wording that whilst schools must fulfil their statutory duties in relation to special needs, 'it is up to them how to do so' (p. i).

The Code of Practice also exhorts schools to formulate a whole-school policy for SEN which is effectively 'owned' by all participants. But the Code gives only general guidance as to how schools should formulate it. It suggests that 'While the governing body and the headteacher will take overall responsibility for the school's SEN policy, the school as a whole should be involved in its development' (p. 8). To allow for the involvement of the whole school in policy formulation is to accept that there will be a time-constraint involved, as Bines (1989) has indicated. This difficulty has been confirmed in a recent small-scale sample of SEN teachers, who argued that the time factor was their most serious concern when attempting to implement the Code (Garner, 1994a). Regrettably, as the Advisory Centre for Education (ACE) (1994b) has indicated, this worry is widespread. Lack of available time for teachers to debate, formulate and implement policy has been a familiar source of unease in recent years (Butt, 1986). This factor alone may well derail the good intentions of both the Code of Practice and other, related, DfE guidance.

There can be little doubt that the main responsibility for the effective implementation of the Code of Practice rests with the SEN Coordinator (now popularly referred to as a SENCO). His or her duties, according to the Code, are extensive, and include a number of new responsibilities, including the formulation of Individual Education Plans (IEPs) (p. 28), suggesting that the coordinator's role is now accepted as pivotal (Simmons, 1994). However, there is a developing view that, in the absence of resources being made available, it is unlikely that he or she will be *able* to be responsible for managing the new procedures because of lack of time. ACE (1994b) is forthright about this, adding that 'the bureaucracy and paperwork that will be required (threaten) to bring the worst features of the '81 Act assessment procedures – bureaucracy and delay – down to school level' (p. 12).

The Code of Practice does not make 'hard and fast rules' (p. 52) in relation to the identification of SEN. Much of the evidence contributing to the identification of a pupil with SEN suggests that it will be gathered subjectively, according to the arrangements current in a given school. Thus, in identifying a learning difficulty, schools must provide evidence of 'impaired social interaction . . . or a significantly restricted repertoire of activities, interests and imaginative development' (p. 55). How are judgements about these attributes to be made, given that each is notoriously open to personal interpretation? In assessing the category of emotional and behavioural difficulties (EBD) a similar dilemma obtains. What, for instance, constitutes 'unpredictable, bizarre, obsessive, violent or severely disruptive behaviour' (p. 59)? The SEN teacher will have considerable responsibility for awareness-raising of these controversial matters.

Sadly, the Code of Practice gives very little advice concerning the day-to-day work that teachers do with children who have SEN. Considerable emphasis is placed upon the importance of the IEP. The concept of IEPs as a 'proactive plan rather than a retrospective record' (Butt and Scott, 1994) is a relatively new idea in mainstream SEN provision, and those faced with designing and implementing them need to be given in-service training to ensure their success. It is significant that the full title of the Code of Practice omits mention of the word 'provision'. It may be that DfE is discreetly implying that identification and assessment are the easy (and low-cost) parts of the SEN equation. Actual provision, whether in terms of human resources, curriculum materials and equipment, and in-service training, is far more costly; another source of heartache for teachers.

The extensive duties to be fulfilled by the SEN Coordinator have already been mentioned. From a practical point of view a query must surely be raised concerning the extent to which teaching time might be affected by her additional duties. As Gains (1994) has implied, 'The role conceived for this group of teachers is breathtakingly broad'. He proceeds to outline eight separate functions for the coordinator, each with specific duties, and can find, within these, only one function that directly involves them in the process of teaching and learning. Could it be, therefore, that the Code of Practice is simply bureaucratising a group of experienced SEN teachers, effectively reducing the amount of time they spend with their pupils?

Finally, practical matters of liaison between schools and support agencies are overlooked in the Code of Practice. The importance of these activities is emphasised at various points in the guidance. But little is made of the difficulties which many schools are now facing following the Education Reform Act. These have been summarised by Bowe and Ball (1992). Whilst the Code suggests that 'Effective action on behalf of children with special educational needs will often depend upon close cooperation between schools, LEAs, the health services and the social services departments of local authorities' (p. 15) there is a real concern that such good intentions may be undermined by the financial pressures faced by these services. Recent evidence (NUT, 1993) indicates that there has been considerable contraction in the resources of many support agencies. As their involvement in SEN work is viewed as fundamental (Gregory, 1989), this decline in available provision may constitute a fatal flaw in the Code.

WORRYING ABOUT THE SIX-PACK: 'TEACHERS WITH PROBLEMS'

In May 1994 the Department for Education (DfE) issued a set of six consultation papers grouped under the heading 'Pupils with Problems'. These were subsequently published with few amendments (DfE, 1994) and offered teachers guidance on, amongst other matters, pupil behaviour, emotional and behavioural difficulties and exclusions. They have now become popularly known as 'the six-pack'. Most teachers have a vested interest in the continuing debate concerning standards of discipline in schools, to which the circulars relating to 'pupils with problems' have contributed, as in the past they have been heavily criticised because of a perceived decline in standards of behaviour in schools.

The Office of Standards in Education (OFSTED) inspection schedule introduced in 1993 highlights the importance of 'discipline' and 'behaviour management' as indicators of effective schools. Elsewhere there is an accepted belief that the level of 'problem behaviour' by pupils in a school is a factor which can be used to judge the climate or ethos of the institution (Cooper, 1993). Exclusions are a particularly important consideration in this respect, in that they provide evidence of how a school is coping with its most difficult pupils.

For most practising teachers the task of classroom management has remained a focus of concern. One difficulty is that individual teachers and schools are inclined to interpret a child's behaviour in different ways. They also adopt widely differing strategies to deal with the problems they encounter. Typical of the dilemmas raised by this state of affairs is the recent debate surrounding 'assertive discipline' (Canter, 1976). Those who support this approach recommend that 'teachers should *not* attempt to deal with pupils' "disturbance" but should get on with the main task for which they are trained and for which they are paid, namely teaching' (Bush and Hill, 1993). To do this they use a series of rewards and punishments operated on strict behaviourist lines. Objectors to this approach argue that its application – particularly in the way advocated by Canter – denies both dignity and rights to the misbehaving child.

PUPIL-INTERESTS, RIGHTS AND THE TEACHER

There has been a growing interest in the rights of individual pupils during the last few years. Child-centred educationists have been seen as influential in this relatively new development, and there is currently a significant growth in the literature in this field. Moreover, some practices adopted by schools, following the advice of the Elton Report (1989), have encouraged more significant participation by pupils whose behaviour is regarded as inappropriate. This group has been amongst the most marginalised and disenfranchised group of pupils in schools (Schostak, 1983).

The Code of Practice relating to special educational needs (DfE, 1994) has sought to build on these developments. The Code states that steps should be taken to 'take into account the ascertainable wishes of the child concerned' (p. 3). Moreover, it goes on to reinforce the principles of both the Children Act (1989) and the UN Convention on the Rights of the Child (1991) by indicating a belief that children can provide 'important and relevant information' and that they 'have a right to be heard' (p. 14). Moreover, there is an explicitly stated belief that pupils should be involved in decision-making (p. 15). Significantly, however, Circular 10/94 (DfE, 1994) in dealing with exclusions makes little or no overt mention of the role of 'problem pupils' in the decision-making processes of the school.

Those involved in SEN have an important role to play in promoting the rights of those children they work with. This, on occasions, can lead to some uncomfortable situations, as they strive to balance their relationships with colleagues (who may not feel committed to the principle of advocacy and self-advocacy) and their allegiance to the child. Moreover, in promoting the rights of pupils it is likely that a range of additional dilemmas will face the teacher (Garner and Sandow, 1995). Each of these concerns has to be dealt with.

WORKING WITH OTHERS . . . IS IT WORKING?

The Court Committee (1976) and the Working Party chaired by Younghusband (1970) had each confirmed that children's needs are best met by a multi-professional approach, characterised by interdisciplinary collaboration. There followed significant developments in special education after the 1981 Education Act in England when cooperation between teachers and those working in the supporting professions were built into the statutory process (Goodwin, 1983). As a result, there is now a considerable body of literature in SEN relating to this style of intervention (Davie, 1993), with cooperative endeavours, in the fields of truancy, child abuse and delinquency being widely publicised. More recently, the Code of Practice (DfE, 1994) has outlined specific guidelines for the continuation of this type of work.

In spite of this both teachers and social workers have faced considerable practical problems in maintaining such a cooperative stance. Lacey and Lomas (1993), for example, whilst acknowledging the importance of multi-disciplinary intervention, stress that it has been very difficult to achieve and that 'It is relatively easy to argue for a unified approach to the needs of children, but quite another for this to happen in practice'. Indeed, Tomlinson (1982) implied that those involved in SEN work have held inappropriately high expectations for this type of collaboration, noting that such practice 'assumes an unrealistic degree of communication, cooperation and absence of professional conflicts and jealousies'.

There are a number of reasons for this state of affairs. The period after the 1988 Education Reform Act (ERA) in England has witnessed a massive increase in teacher-workload, particularly in respect of recording and assessment. In consequence teachers have been unable to devote sufficient time to liaison activity with supporting professionals. Similar constraints undoubtedly operate on social workers. There is also evidence of 'innovation fatigue' in both education in general, and special education in particular (Bines, 1993). Hardly a month goes by without a major policy initiative on the part of government. Many teachers have been increasingly unable to keep pace with these demands, as the burgeoning levels of stress-related absences from work have shown.

This points increasingly towards a paradox. On the one hand, inter-agency cooperation is viewed as essential for the successful outcome of any intervention with children who are at risk. This is confirmed by the rhetoric contained in DfE guidance concerning 'Pupils with Problems' (DfE, 1994), for example. At the same time, however, those involved in the education of children who have SEN have consistently had to argue for increased resources to enable cooperative work to continue (Diamond, 1993). This has not been forthcoming, from successive governments, and there is little evidence of change in the foreseeable future (Mittler, 1993). At the same time the increase in incidence of children who have SEN and of child poverty, undeniably linked to the incidence of SEN, as reported by the CPAG (1995), continues, and the infrastructures to meet their educational and social needs show signs of collapsing under the strain of funding cutbacks (Bangs, 1993).

SEPARATE PROVISION

This book deals with SEN in a holistic way. It is now fashionable to talk in terms of 'inclusive education', and there is justification in the cynical view of some of those teachers working in special schools that such terminology simply disguises inadequate provision. They would argue that until SEN receives an appropriate level of funding, which will ensure that all children can receive the educational experiences they are entitled to, the ideology of integration is spurious and self-serving. It is by no means certain that such an approach meets the educational needs of all children. Typical of this kind of posturing is the view presented by Booth (1994), who states that 'a properly resourced mainstream can replace most special schools'.

'Mainstreaming' has been in the ascendancy since the Warnock era, and few would argue that it is not the right of every child to experience education in such a setting. The role of special schools has, on the other hand, been the subject of considerable debate, with some authors suggesting that these schools are 'under siege', being 'caught in a crossfire between the forces of equity and excellence' (Chapman, 1994).

We are going to resist the temptation to debate this controversial matter in more detail. Rather, we would ask the reader to recognise that each of our contributing teachers, whether they work within mainstream or special schools, has to deal almost on a daily basis with the dilemmas that result. In doing so they are bringing to the attention of the educational community as a whole that 'excellence' and 'effectiveness', those favourite words of educational pundits, can take many forms and be possible in widely different contexts. As Florek (1986) observed, 'Integration is *not* about closing down special schools. It is about developing special education regardless of its particular location. Integration is *not* about changing the concept of special education, only its context'.

DEALING WITH LEGISLATION: ERA AND ALL THAT

The Education Reform Act brought about a number of significant changes to the way in which SEN was organised. Amongst them, three concerns have been a consistent source of debate amongst teachers working with children who have learning difficulty: the changes to curriculum organisation, as a result of the introduction of the National Curriculum, the introduction of Local Management of Schools, and open enrolment and parental choice.

The National Curriculum (NC), even in its post-Dearing form, presents a number of concerns to those working with children who have learning difficulties. The NC is essentially a product-based curriculum model, with its objectives, attainment targets and frequent assessments of performance. Illustrative of this approach is the advice contained in a 'Curriculum for All' (NCC, 1989), which states that 'it will be found that some attainment targets can be broken down more easily than others into smaller steps'.

Many (if not most) teachers are drawn to work in SEN because they subscribe to the belief that children learn best in a creative, enquiry-led and open-ended manner, best summarised as a 'process approach'. This allows them to address the needs of the whole child and recognises that most learning difficulties cannot easily be ascribed to a simple cause or manifestation. As

Blenkin, Edwards and Kelly (1992) state, such an approach 'does not predetermine what pupils are to learn or the forms of behaviour they are to acquire. Rather it seeks to create the conditions under which they can grow and develop as individual autonomous beings'. The differences between this approach and the product-led arrangements of the NC provide fertile ground for teachers to continue the debate into the next century, and to innovate according to their affiliations.

Whilst many teachers would agree with Charlesworth's (1990) early analysis that there are more advantages than disadvantages in LMS, others would subscribe to the type of comments reported by Doyle and Rickman (1989) in opposing such moves as moving education towards a market-orientation in which children with SEN will be the principal losers. LMS has remained a contentious issue amongst those working in SEN. As schools have assumed direct control over their budgets, teachers and parents expressed worries that available funds might be insufficient to provide the necessary level of support to children, irrespective of whether they possess a statement of SEN. As Doyle and Rickman point out, 'What has become apparent to us, on reflection, is that . . . special educational needs are, almost of necessity, becoming a low priority in planning at school level'. They argue that teachers ought to 'examine seriously the possible and probable effects of LMS on schools where cost effectiveness, marketing and competition may if unchallenged become the primary concern of headteachers'.

Elsewhere Peter (1989) raises a series of further dilemmas which form a backdrop to teachers' working lives. Amongst these are the difficulty of ensuring that mainstream SEN provision is adequately safeguarded, the need to guarantee earmarked funds to employ support staff, and the pervasive effects of formula funding, which may seriously affect schools in inner cities with a high proportion of children who have SEN.

Finally, the ongoing inequalities in provision between different LEAs and regions in England and Wales means that the quality of educational provision for children with learning difficulties has become a lottery. This is especially so as the effects of open-enrolment become more widespread. Schools are now free to accept children on to their roll from a much wider catchment than hitherto. As the education of children who have SEN is relatively expensive, some schools may seek to restrict the numbers of such children on their rolls (Lunt, 1990). Schools can also be more selective as to the children they choose to admit. This has serious implications for children who have SEN, and especially for those who have emotional and/or behavioural difficulties. Some critics have even argued that such a system is bound to create 'sink' schools, with high concentrations of SEN.

CONCLUSION

Teachers working in the field of SEN have to address, in some shape or form, most, if not all, of the matters outlined above. What must be remembered is that they have to deal with these issues whilst going about their daily work with children. They have to rationalise, in their own minds, the inequities and inadequacies of the education system in which they work so that maximum benefits accrue to the children they are committed to. The remainder of this book tells us something of the way in which they manage it.

SECTION 1

1

What Teachers Think

In our introduction we outlined a number of concerns affecting the working lives of teachers in special education. We argued that they had to operate in the context of considerable and ongoing educational change which, in turn, has a major influence on defining the principles and professional perspectives which govern the work they do. Our purpose in this chapter is to explore the thoughts of teachers who work with children who have SEN, in order to uncover some of the assumptions about the nature and purpose of their special education practice. How teachers *think* may be placed in a critical position in developing successful classroom practitioners; and as such it is central to the role of reflective practice.

It is not the purpose of this chapter to establish arguments for the primacy of reflection in teaching in general, for this has been accomplished in considerable detail elsewhere (Schon, 1983; Pollard and Tann, 1991, etc.). What is notable is that teachers who are involved in SEN work have, in recent years, had little opportunity to engage in the kind of critical thinking about their area of interest, mainly because of the pressures resulting from the need to implement change. This is not to say, of course, that teachers don't think; rather, that they are seldom given the breathing space to do so within the course of their teaching day.

Teachers who work in the field of SEN have been regarded, like the children they interact with, as 'different'. One reason for this view is that, because most teachers working in SEN recognise the powerful relationship between special education and issues of equity, fairness and social justice, they have developed an intense cynicism towards an education system which is perceived as being manifestly unequal, unfair and lacking in social justice. As a result such teachers' perceptions of their role, about the work that they do, and about the children they come in contact with, is heavily underpinned by a healthily cynical and reactive stance to many of the educational changes (it would be difficult to call them 'reforms') proposed or introduced by central or regional government. SEN teachers are critical by nature, and that, according to the principles of reflective practice, is root and branch to the professional actions that they subsequently take in classrooms and schools.

The chapter is therefore about the instinctive reactions and thinking of

3

teachers on a range of matters concerning SEN. Although the reader will notice some broad correlations between the context for SEN that we have mapped in the initial chapter, we have purposely tried not to place too constraining a structure on the written thoughts contained in the chapter. Whilst we have selected some themes, our belief is that 'what teachers think' about SEN issues will have an individual coherence and logic for each reader, and be reinforced in many of the subsequent sections of the book.

MAPPING THE CONCERNS

To provide some initial illustrations of this we will draw upon the work of some teachers who were asked to represent their thoughts about their job in a graphical way. This group of teachers were invited to construct a 'concept map', a mind-map, which gave the unfamiliar observer a set of information about their position as special needs teachers in school. The teachers were also asked to write a brief statement explaining why they had represented their work in the way that they had.

The use of concept maps is not yet widespread. Its value is in prompting teachers to think in an alternative dimension. Buzan (1988) states that it is a method guided by the principle that 'Rather than starting from the top and working down in sentences or lists, one should start from the centre or main idea and branch out as dictated by the individual ideas and general form of the central theme'.

Because it does this it often provides quite powerful, often unacknowledged, scenarios about what their work entails and the conflicting demands made on them. It represents the value of letting 'ideas pour forth without censorship or deliberation' (Goldberg, 1989). Let us look at some examples.

R. C.'s concept map (Figure 1), although simple and apparently lacking in detail, provides a wealth of information and insight into the perceptions of a support teacher in a primary school. What it tells us is that the role of the SEN Coordinator (SENCO) is seen as indeterminate in its areas of responsibilities. Some indication of the breadth of work required of SENCOs is contained in her accompanying description:

although the SENCO has to do all the bull-work, the real power and authority is vested in the headteacher who decides what course of action is to be taken . . . though the SENCO has the responsibilty for ensuring that the class-teachers are having no problem with SEN children either in respect of curriculum differentiation or monitoring and assessing their progress, she has to rely heavily on the headteacher for her support.

It appears to me that our organisation has a very tall structure for a small infant school . . . there exists a great deal of bureaucracy . . . The hierarchy of office is quite well defined in our school. I think there is a lot of responsibility vested in the SENCO (but) there is not enough support and time provided for the efficient delivery of her duties . . . as a result class-teachers and the child

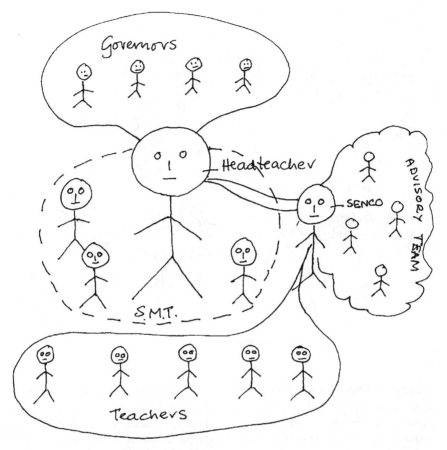

Figure 1   Concept map – the role of the SENCO

with SEN suffer. It would definitely help if we had a more 'collegial' organisational system, where all the teachers are involved.

The concept map illustrated in Figure 2 has been drawn by a mainstream secondary-school teacher who works as an SEN teacher who also teaches some history. Although the teacher presented this set of concepts without an accompanying commentary, it is able to stand on its own as a stark reminder that the SEN teacher has a complex set of relationships to maintain if she is to fulfil her required function. Barton (1991) argues that such a balance cannot be secured if the conditions under which teachers have to work are unsatisfactory.

  If we consider this concept map in these terms we can see that the teachers who work mainly with children who have learning difficulty have a host of conflicting allegiances. They must interact with colleagues from elsewhere in the school, whilst at the same time being seen by some as occupying a less than

Figure 2   Concept map – the role of the SEN teacher

stressful position within the school – are they proper teachers? The children demand attention, and they have to decide how to prioritise this help, whilst those of their colleagues who do not view them cynically compete in the same way for their input. And within the SEN department of the school there are a multitude of jobs that need to be done, which erode the conditions in which these teachers work and, over time, reduces their effectiveness (Apple, 1986).

Other concept maps are equally revealing. D. S., who works in a mainstream secondary school, points out that, whilst special needs staff wish to 'welcome' other professionals and to interact with them, they are constrained by a series of pressures which forces them to behave defensively (Figure 3). He writes that

The diagram I drew . . . depicts a castle, with a sign of welcome above the door. However, the 'portcullis' (gateway) is firmly closed, and those that are inside the castle are having to defend themselves against the following factors (depicted surrounding the castle):
- the constraints of budgets – (cost neutrality of the Code of Practice)
- hostility from pupils who are afraid of their poor image whilst receiving in-class or withdrawal support
- hostile views and suspicion of other teaching staff
- requirements imposed by the Local Education Authority
- workload of the Code of Practice
- hostile views of parents

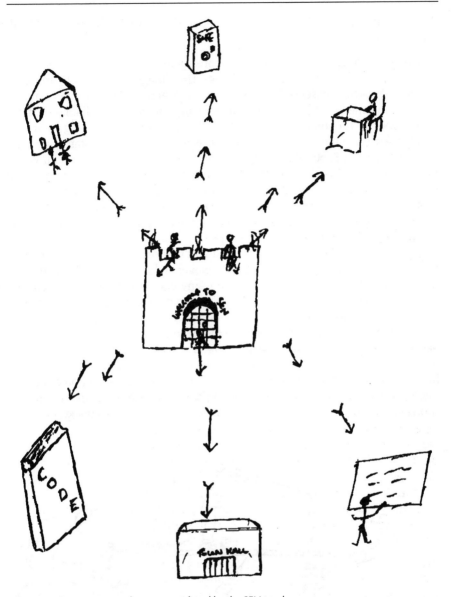

Figure 3 Concept map – the pressures faced by the SEN teacher

All of these aspects are part of the job of managing a special educational needs department, but detract from the real role of the staff involved, which is to teach those children who have learning difficulties.

Nor are these kinds of issues restricted to mainstream schools. F. W. works in a Pupil Referral Unit (PRU) and offers the following account which vividly illustrates that the tensions facing teachers working in SEN are apparent in all types of provision.

When asked to represent the management structure of my workplace it wasn't difficult to think of an image. (Figure 4) This image reflects both my own feelings towards the school and I believe the actual state of affairs at this moment in time (1/3/95). The unit has recently undergone a change of status from a Special Technical Centre to a Pupil Referral Unit. This change involved a tightening up of the management structure and an increase in staff numbers. I was taken on last September along with one other new member of staff. While the place was an STC I get the impression that the emphasis was on preparing the pupils for a life of practical, manual work and very little teaching of the academic with the exception of the three 'Rs'. This changed when the unit became a PRU with the same status as a school and now much more time is spent teaching national curriculum subjects.

When an STC each member of the staff was fairly autonomous and each had final say in their particular area, however when things changed, this arrangement changed as well. The rope in my diagram represents the current status of the unit (the label reads 'new'). The two people at either end are two of the original members of staff, one of whom is now the centre's head teacher and the other who *thinks* he should be the head but is actually one of the two deputy heads. As the rope suggests there is a great deal of tension between them and to pull in opposite directions is about all they can agree on. The history of this situation pre-dates my arrival so I cannot comment other than to say that it adds extra spice to the working day. However I feel that the unit is strong enough to stand this tension which is why the rope is so thick.

Figure 4   Concept map – a management structure

On the rope is the other new member of staff, the second deputy head. He has taken on a conciliatory role between the two staff mentioned above while at the same time balancing the interests of the other staff, he is my point of contact with the rest of management and is very helpful in that respect which is why the line (which represents that help) has knots in it. From the balance bar hangs the last member of the original staff, the administrative assistant who also does some teaching. She is in roughly the same relation to the senior management as I am but has a more stable base than I because she has been at the centre longer. We support each other for, as she says, when there are so many Chiefs, the Indians have to stick together, so the image of the balance bar between us represents mutual support and not distance.

Hanging from the knotted rope is me, with one foot on the climb towards management responsibilities and eager to get there, but aware that it may be a difficult journey. I'm looking out of the picture because I know that I am being assessed by people outside of the centre (in the LEA) who are keen that I should do well. Around this structure orbit the children, bruised and battered by the changes that they have gone through since September and never making contact as far as the management structure is concerned.

This then is the management system of my workplace, as I see and understand it now. I feel slightly like an outsider, mainly because I am not used to being this close to higher management and feel a bit exposed. I am trying to make sense of what I see and to tread my way carefully through the management minefield. I am hoping that learning about management will help me to succeed.

The graphic representations provided here as an introduction to this chapter highlight a complex pattern of concerns and pressures facing teachers in the field of SEN. It is very apparent that a career in any branch of special education has become more complicated than hitherto. Teachers go into battle on a daily basis knowing that, in the absence of sufficient time and resources they have had to become skilled in the art of prioritisation. As one teacher explained, she has now to juggle many conflicting role-requirements, given that 'Each week some new priorities occur. The goal posts just seem to change. Each day/week unfolds new drama where through interaction with different people I learn something new and understand something old better.' (R. C.)

What is remarkable is that teachers still manage to accomplish the things they do.

PERSONAL HISTORIES AND PROFESSIONAL ACTIVITY

The role of the teacher is marked by a series of role tensions. In order to function effectively it is necessary for teachers to find some equation or at least a nominal balance between their own acknowledged personal needs within teaching and the pragmatic nature of much of their own professional activity and development. The two things cannot really be separated. Part of what makes a teacher feel 'good' about the work she does is the knowledge that her involvement with a child who has SEN is having a material effect on his educational performance, and most probably his life. The sense of well-being generated in this way is in equal parts personal and professional.

Both personal and professional matters help to construct the identity of a teacher, which is formed by the sum of personal self-concepts, value-systems and personal and professional circumstances (MacLure, 1993). For the SEN teacher in the 1990s, as we have outlined, personal and professional need is conditioned by the wider events in education, and by the effects of central government policy on a wide range of other matters, from economics to welfare. Intrinsic commitment is conditioned by pragmatism for the sake of career progression.

Our argument, shared by many involved in teacher-development in SEN, is that, by understanding something of what comprises this personal/professional interface, teachers involved in SEN work will be better placed to rationalise their own actions. By so doing they will be refining a professional identity and sense of 'self'.

Teachers come to the classroom with a variety of recollections from their past concerning special needs. In all probability matters relating to disability and learning difficulty were dealt with very differently in their own childhood. L. P., for example, observes that

My parents' attitudes were humanitarian. I would never have been allowed to show unkindness to someone less well off than myself. When I was older, at secondary school, I saw a girl with Down's syndrome waiting for her school minibus; I laughed at her, and nudged my friend, who told me 'people like that never forgot a face, they were really strong and would come after me'. A magical model. Her attitude stirred up fear and suspicion in me.

Sadly, however, some of these early experiences are still replicated now. Identifying such attitudes by biographical recall can be helpful in dealing with contemporary manifestation of such beliefs. This example, for instance, allows consideration of the historical derivation of SEN. Whilst a normative history of special education would have us believe that disability linked to sorcery, witchcraft and the wrath of God is an interpretation drawn from the Middle Ages, from Victorian England and from the fertile minds of ideological spin-doctors, L. P. draws from the near past to provide evidence that more work has yet to be done: many of those teachers from her secondary school, whilst not subscribing to the demonic attitudes evinced in her description, are still practising teachers. What is their sense of attitudinal recall now? There is a sneaking worry or cynicism, that a veneer of political correctness may have overtaken many teachers, who have now to recognise the rights of those children who have SEN. In the past there was no such compunction, as O. C. confirms: I remember '. . . the headmaster telling all of us, at Assembly, that we must pray for those children less fortunate than us and that the Kelly family wouldn't be at school for the next two weeks. Years later I was told he'd ended up in prison.'

Dealing with attitudes on a personal level by recalling events from a teacher's own experiences as a pupil in school can also reinforce the conviction felt towards working in SEN. It also helps to preserve balance, in that it convinces us that inequality and disadvantage, both clearly implicated in the incidence of restricted educational opportunity and SEN amongst certain groups, are not new creations, beasts spawned by the excesses of a market economy. Again, O. C. recalls the following occasion from her time as a pupil:

My next memory is at a junior school where there was a family of several children, Irish, very poorly dressed, noisy and always in trouble with teachers. We had Reggie in our class. He was tall, well built with tight blond curls. His trousers and jumpers were always too short and he never wore shoes, only plimsolls. Our teacher spent a lot of time shouting at Reggie, who never finished his work, always made mistakes and crossings out and never stopped talking to the other boys. One day the teacher, to 'shame' him, put him at the front with the girls and he sat next to me. All I can remember was an overwhelming smell of ammonia and telling him to 'shut up!'.

N. P. offers another example of the way in which the recollections from a teacher's own experience as a pupil can be used to illustrate contemporary constraints and possibilities. After a period of hospitalisation, N. P. returned to her primary school, and her parents asked that she should be treated as 'normal'. N. explains that

the children felt I was different because I disappeared now and again, and could leave the class to go to the toilet whenever I wanted to. I wasn't pushed to complete work when they were, because I had missed some school and was allowed to have more time. Looking back this was because some teachers thought I wasn't as capable as the others because I was sick. Of course, my condition had nothing to do with my mental capability, but possibly they were working on the assumption that because I was physically ill I was somehow slower at using my brain.

N. P.'s comments reveal something about how children who have a special need can receive a narrow educational experience. This is not necessarily because of any perverse intent on the part of teachers, as the above example shows. N.P.'s teachers wanted to offer her protection, and were concerned that, if pushed too hard, she might have become ill again. What the passage does illustrate is the importance of cooperation between the professions, a matter which is explored in a number of places in this book.

R. S., too, provides an honest account of her childhood response to disability. In the following extract she compares her past experience with those of today, illustrating how there has been an attitudinal shift for many people – a situation from which we can draw encouragement but not complacency:

As a Girl Guide I remember visiting an institution where there were Downs syndrome and autistic children. I had to spend two days with them for a badge and it was a real endurance test. I felt very uncomfortable because I had never been with such people. I think I looked down on them as lesser mortals, being thankful that I was not like them. They were outside my experience and I could not understand how the adults who cared for them could give them so much affection. Even as a Cadet Guider when a girl with MS joined us I felt she was different and just could not treat her as a normal person. I think that some of my friends were also relieved when she left. I now have two good friends with MS and I know a dear boy with cerebral palsy. I think it is ignorance which breeds fear.

What these accounts imply is that all teachers bring something of their history to the classroom encounter, and this undoubtedly affects their approach to SEN, a job which C. J. describes as 'taking up a lot of time and energy, a lot of which does seem pointless', given that 'my authority is restricted by lack of experience and undermining from the head of department'. Teachers must analyse their personal responses to professional situations in order to make sense of what they are participating in.

One way in which teachers following INSET courses have been encouraged to do this is by utilising the 'Johari Window' (Luft and Ingram, 1955), which allows them to explore the ways in which they present to others, as well as providing insights into those personal attributes which, although important in their role-functioning, often remain 'hidden' from their colleagues. Here, for example, C. J. readily admits that 'I often feel very insecure in my role but cannot allow that to show to other staff or pupils. I must appear confident.' Recognising feelings about professional situations can be very challenging, as 'Past history, fragile egos, excessive interference, unprofessionalism and unco-operation all make life very difficult' (C. J.).

This approach also allows teachers to examine the 'blind spot' that most of us have, to a greater or lesser degree, thereby providing a further way of discovering what our colleagues think of us. In attempting to establish what are the features of this part of our personal 'window', it is important to remember that reflection *on* practice is at its most effective when others are allowed to participate in the process in a supportive way. But, however encouraging colleagues can be, receiving opinions from other teachers about the work we do can be immensely threatening. Again, C. J. illustrates this: 'I would hope that my immediate colleagues and friends would tell me if something I did affected a pupil in an adverse way. All the support staff trust each other and we must be able to encourage when good results occur and give feedback if adverse things happen.'

In a later chapter we consider some of the ways in which this high level of self-scrutiny and analysis is utilised by those participating in INSET. This way of thinking is particularly crucial to the development of reflection in professional development, again a topic which we examine in more detail in the closing section of this book. At this stage, however, and as a means of locating 'what teachers think' as a central component of effective INSET, it is worth recalling the observation of Elliott (1991) that

From the perspective of the 'reflective practitioner' model professional competence consists of the ability to act intelligently in situations which are sufficiently novel and unique to require what constitutes an appropriate response to be learned in situ. Competence cannot be defined in terms of an ability to apply pre-ordained categories of specialist knowledge to produce correct behavioural responses.

ACCOUNTABILITY AND WORKING WITH OTHERS

Teachers involved in SEN work are deeply conscious of the need to balance demands on their time and expertise from a wide range of individuals. At a micro-level, in the classroom, the way in which a teacher makes sense of the needs of all pupils has become both an integral part of SEN practice (as illustrated elsewhere in this book) and also a constant focus of teachers' thinking. Thankfully, even during a period of considerable pressure to adopt a more commercial view of SEN (one thinks at this point, with some cynicism, of the 'business units' which are now central to SEN operations in many LEAs) specialist teachers have retained their integrity by continuing to place emphasis upon the work they do with the children themselves. This commitment is apparent in many of their statements concerning how they perceive 'accountability'.

As mentioned in the previous chapter, the level of public and professional accountability brings with it a high level of role-uncertainty, de-skilling and stress. Many involved in SEN work are highly self-critical of their performance, even though they do their job under extremely arduous conditions. B. A., for instance, expresses dissatisfaction at the way in which a particular part of his teaching week had gone:

I didn't feel satisfied with the aims I set for myself in terms of the children. I felt that in some ways the children took a back seat to the academic work and admin-istrative work even though they were the first on my list. This needs to be changed.

This personal soul-searching is a salient feature of daily accounts provided by SEN teachers, and within these there is evidence of deep and widespread examination of what factors lie behind the decisions made on account of children who have SEN. P. Q. suggests that, in the educational encounters which she has experienced, all is not what it seems, and that those involved in SEN have to re-examine what they do in order that they don't fall into the trap of stereotyping or of recognising that 'underachievement' is axiomatic to the child with a learning difficulty:

there are two sides to every story and that invariably when dealing with youngsters within my school I must remember that my main priority is to treat them with dignity and respect. However, there are times especially in hindsight that my reactions and responses have been very judgemental and have not always taken the child's viewpoint into consideration.

Some of the descriptions provided by the teachers whose work forms the basis of this book provide graphic accounts of the range of individuals and agencies, with the accompanying guidance and legislation, who need to be taken into account in the day-to-day work that they do. They each provide appropriate testimony to the view of Humphreys and Sturt (1993) that

An establishment needs high levels of stability and maturity to cope with even limited innovation; the timescale of National Curriculum implementation can lead to high levels of innovation fatigue in even stable institutions. In institutions which are themselves undergoing internal conflict or reorganisation, the pace of change can lead to disturbing levels of extra stress among staff.

Accounts of the range of weekly duties completed by the teachers can be found in the next section. They represent snapshots of teachers' day-to-day existence. W. L. recalls Becker's (1970) analysis, when he

defined three areas within which teachers are accountable: professional (to one's colleagues), contractual (to one's employer) and moral (to one's pupils). These three areas would present many audiences, and those I will address are: school and colleagues, governors, LEA, parents, pupils and oneself.

It is indicative of the complexities of the work of the SEN professional that the successful operation of each of these could be said to constitute a full-time role in its own right. In the following sections, we illustrate some of these roles.

THINKING ABOUT THE CODE OF PRACTICE

Much of the material for this volume has been collected at a time when the Code of Practice remained in its draft form. Nevertheless, it is noteworthy that there were already indications that teachers were adopting the same high level of scrutiny to this DfE guidance as they had devoted to other issues involved in SEN. As we note at various points in this book, this kind of reflection, about both principles and practice, is fundamental to the development of the kind of personal responses which are critical to effective teaching. In fact, it has been given additional credibility by managers and policy-makers, who 'can therefore claim both administrative and humanitarian grounds for taking an interest in the personal dimension of workers lives' (MacLure, 1989).

The Code of Practice, by the very nature of its coverage of SEN matters and their implications for all teachers, will assume a central place in this reflection. There has been an immediate recognition of its likely impact on the managerial role of those involved in SEN. L. G., for instance, confirms that 'Because of the new Code of Practice, I can foresee that the management of special needs could have a much more important part to play in the management structure of the school and school life as a whole'.

The same teacher expands on this observation:

The role of the SENCO is going to become more and more important, in particular as a liaison between the school, agencies and parents . . . This is becoming very time consuming already – particularly when trying to phone agencies who may only be available at certain times. I think some of the SENCO's most important attributes will need to be tact and patience, when trying to keep everybody happy and informed, while dealing with many different personalities all wanting and expecting different things.

Specific parts of the Code will become the focus of detailed critiques by teachers. One area of discussion and controversy will undoubtedly be the newly expanded role of the SENCO, as L. G. has indicated in the above extract. A similarly contentious issue will be the design and operation of individual education plans (IEPs), which some have already seen as counter-productive and overly bureaucratic: 'However, the danger of individual learning programmes lies in the management problems generated for teachers who are unable to spend extended periods of time talking individually with all young people' (G. K.).

Elsewhere in this chapter we have noted a number of teachers' comments concerning working with others. This, too, may prove to be a problematic area in the operation of the Code, given the lack of time currently available for liaison work:

In the light of the new Code of Practice we are trying to tighten up our procedures to ensure that the children get the best help possible. With so many people involved with one child, it is extremely important that all are prepared to discuss, listen and share skills and expertise. There is always the danger of professional jealousy so it has to be recognised that everyone has a contribution to make and that the welfare of the child should always be the first concern. (L.G.)

As the Code of Practice pays specific and detailed attention to the assessment of SEN, it is interesting to note one teacher's response to this important area. L. C., who works as a support teacher, raises the following questions:

1. Do pupils carry out recording of work?
2. Is the work produced in keeping with the teacher's reasonable expectation of the pupil's abilities?
3. Are grades/marks consistent?
4. What kind of tests or grading system is being used?
5. What kind of provision is made for the 'Quality Audit'?
6. How is information provided to others outside the school?

THINKING ABOUT BEHAVIOUR

Teachers arguably spend as much time thinking about, and discussing, the social behaviour of children in school as they do about the teaching and learning that goes on in connection with the formal, academic curriculum. This is hardly surprising, given that one of the prerequisites for effective instruction is a well-behaved class which spends more time on-task. For those involved with children who have learning difficulties the correlation between problem behaviour and underachievement has become a widely accepted relationship. This point has been forcibly made by both the Elton Report (DES, 1989) and by Circular 8/94, relating to pupil behaviour and discipline, and is given a high priority in the existing school inspection schedule (OFSTED, 1993). But it is also fair to say that many teachers are preoccupied with the behaviour of children because of the (mistaken) criticism, orchestrated invariably by the media and politicians, that schools in England are descending into indiscipline.

Amplifying these general comments, O. C. remarks that

The school has a policy of differentiation by setting in all subjects apart from English. This results in 'bottom' sets, of up to 32 students, who quite clearly see themselves as 'failures' and whose behaviour reflects this. The problem increases as they go through the school . . . by Year 10 they are aware that they will not be entered for GCSEs and so become non-attenders, and, when they do attend, are disruptive and aggressive.

This leaves little doubt that both academic and social functioning are the parallel concerns of those connected with SEN. For many other teachers in schools it is the case that the disturbing behaviour of the 'problem pupil' is the primary target of attention, rather than the academic underachievement that underpins it. Or, to look at the phenomenon in another way, 'Generally "behaviour" is regarded as an area for punishment, not reward. It is perfectly possible to go right through our school, in bottom sets, achieving absolutely nothing, by remaining quiet and not drawing attention to yourself' (O. C.).

From the commentaries we have gathered, it is also noteworthy that many of the teachers are only too well aware of the political agenda which lies behind the public perception of 'problem behaviour', as the following two extracts show:

I am very conscious of the part played by staff in the whole area of problem behaviour – mainly due to our perceptions of events. With the advent of league tables etc. the pressures on schools are unbearable, performance is the key to everything. However, where do the needs of individuals come in, especially those who have special educational needs which can affect their behaviour? (P. Q.)

'I do feel that in some ways what the Government and Inspectors have to take on board is that exclusions are in some way an expediency which really does little justice to either political ideologies or schools or young people themselves'. (P. Q.)

But there is also a consistent acknowledgement that, in thinking about the behaviour of children, these teachers are having to deal with perhaps the most problematic aspect of SEN provision. The final extracts in this section signal the concerns that two of our contributors have in this respect: 'I feel that I had been caught up in the dangerous process of not separating the disturbing act from the individual' (P. Q.). 'I believe that the major problem is that there is no consistency amongst staff as to what "bad" behaviour is, and therefore students "get away" with certain types of behaviour according to what teacher it is' (O. C.).

CONCLUSION

This chapter is arguably about gut reactions. The remarks made by the teachers on the preceding pages carry a spirit of instinctiveness about them. In doing so they provide an opportunity to examine the concerns of those most closely involved with children with SEN. They are the thoughts which, in all probability, are at the back of the mind even during 'off-duty' times, such is the importance of the issues they focus upon. But it will become equally apparent, from the main body of this book, that most teachers working in this field are conscious of the urgent need to translate such thinking into action.

SECTION 2
Organising and Planning

Introduction

Because the attention of the public is always directed to the role of the teacher in the classroom, most people are quite unaware of the teacher as manager. No teachers nowadays escape the daily grind of organisation, whether of their own work, or of their interactions with others. What is clearly not understood, as witnessed by the publicly expressed contempt for people with a nine to three-thirty working day and long sun-filled holidays, is the degree of detailed planning required, and the range of interpersonal skills involved in dealing with children, other teachers, senior managers, external specialists and parents. Most, if not all, of this is achieved without the allocation of specific hours for the various tasks, a situation unimaginable in industry or commerce.

In this section we concentrate on teachers as organisers, planning their own time, and the time of children in their class or tutor group. We also explore the way in which special needs teachers at different levels have to advocate for individuals and groups of children. The relation of SEN teachers with subject specialists is particularly difficult to negotiate, given the different priorities which inevitably contribute to the dialogue. A particular problem here is the hazy view which some specialist teachers may have of the nature of the difficulty which the child is experiencing. Subject teachers are often said, even by themselves, to be teaching 'geography (or whatever) not children'. The underlying assumption is that readying the children to 'receive' geography is the function of some other teacher, usually at an earlier age, and that the SEN teacher's task is to carry this out for those 'stragglers' who are not ready for the absorption of subject knowledge. Hence for many years, special needs teaching in the secondary sector has been largely confined to basic English and mathematics. Even in the new National Curriculum documents, the advice for teachers in relation to children with SEN does not do more than suggest that they should be offered material 'selected from earlier key stages' in the various subjects.

It is not surprising that the complexity of cognitive, social and emotional development, which may affect in particular and different ways the individual child's response to subject studies, is hard to comprehend. More recently there has been a range of texts published (for example, Wilson, 1985; Clarke and Wigley, 1988) which do help in developing understanding of ways to make subject studies available to the whole school population.

Where support teaching is an accepted part of a school's organisation, it can still only be successful if the negotiated relationship with class or subject teacher is fully understood and agreed. Many teachers feel threatened by the presence of another teacher in the classroom, and the arrangement of duties is a delicate business as seen in Chapter 2. 'Making materials' can seem a usurpation of the class or subject teacher's role, where helping children on an individual basis may not seem so threatening. The question of whether the support teacher is there to support the teacher or the children is often unaddressed. Visser (1986) suggests that the teacher is *implicitly* supported: making this *explicit* may sometimes be counter-productive.

Planning for children may appear an obvious task: however, most planning is done on a whole-class basis, and the planning for individuals intrinsic to the preparation of an individual education programme (IEP) is another task for the SEN specialist. Here, as in other areas, the teacher can draw on the wide experience of special school teaching in which individual planning and programming has long been central.

It is obvious that any one of those concerned with special education perceive their own role as central and the others as peripheral. Teachers are likely to be as egotistical as the rest in this. However, they do have a role as coordinator of a range of inputs, and must be able to negotiate effectively with other professionals and with parents, often in situations where trust is missing and perceptions wide of the mark (Sandow, 1987).

This section thus highlights some of the tasks carried out by teachers which form a significant but often ignored part of their lives.

2

Teachers Organising Themselves

Teaching is an occupation which is amazingly complex. The central task itself has a hundred components. However, just as in the wider world, that main responsibility is only made possible by a considerable amount of organisation and planning. For the teacher who has a special responsibility for supporting children with learning difficulties, the sheer complexity of managing physical and personal resources is hard to comprehend. In the extract below, a mainstream history teacher who also acts as a form tutor in a large comprehensive school is also responsible for acting as a special needs support teacher. She lists the tasks she completes throughout the course of one week in June 1994.

The list should be read with the knowledge that there is no non-contact time allowed for these tasks: (apart from one hour per week for 'making materials') they must be achieved in corridors, at break-times and in other snatched moments.

Priority	Type	Details	Completed?
High	Support (I team teach here) (I regularly make material)	*Adapt materials for bottom set history for Friday 'life as a slave' but check scheme of work. If possible build in some scope for extended writing in response to open-ended questions but need to cater for the three who virtually can't write at all: role-play group work with scribe? Then photocopy the results of group effort?** See the mainstream teacher: will we split the class between us this week, or stay together? Who will lead if the latter?	Not needed; I forgot there would be no lesson on Friday (Sports day) (I did not make any materials this week, unusually)

*Note the teacher takes responsibility for *differentiation of outcomes*. The mainstream teacher is responsible for her class. The support teacher must negotiate her role: this might be difficult if the subject is actually (as in this case) the support teacher's specialism.

Priority	Type	Details	Completed?
High	Mainstream history	*Give Year 8 marks to form tutors on Monday*	Done
High	Form tutor	*See Reprographics and get 30 more Parent Interview forms run off Get pupils to note subject teacher (Tuesday Registration a.m.) Put forms in folder in staffroom*	Done
High	Support (I've only recently started to work with this teacher and have done little English support)	*See English teacher to clarify what we'll do for Tuesday's English lesson for 8 Green. I've forgotten what she told me she'd like me to do. Check if she still prefers that I don't support in the classroom. Check what she said in response to my suggestion that I do a needs analysis of their work in their folders. Can't promise to make any materials this week but could plan. Could provide differentiated spelling patterns for those I've already seen. Easier to do if I come into lesson.**	Several attempts to meet but didn't succeed until a week later. She didn't need me to do anything for Tuesday's lesson as the class were doing something for the school play or something.\n\n13/6 We have now clarified the situation about what I will do. I will monitor and make brief notes on four pupils each session. She will send them to be interviewed by me. I am also not going to offer to make materials at all for English now. No time!

* It appears that negotiation is necessary here too: the mainstream teacher is hesitant about in-class support. Like many others it seems she would prefer the pupils with problems to be withdrawn.

Priority	Type	Details	Completed?
High	Form tutor	*Sort out sportsday competitors and give list to PE Dept*	Done
High	Mainstream history	*Make sure I can do IT newspaper on AppleMac (Personal Press) for Year 8 history next week*	Postponed till next week but got it done
High	Mainstream history	*Mark rest of 7 Orange history exercise books*	Done
High	Mainstream history	*Prepare my regular five mainstream history lessons*	Done
High	Extra English	*Prepare my regular two extra English sessions*	Done

It is clear that SEN is just a part of this teacher's weekly responsibility.

Priority	Type	Details	Completed?
Medium	Extra English and general support	Organise pupils to do some work for me cutting up the differentiated spelling patterns from big sheet. (They get merits as rewards for work done in their own time.)	Started several off. Did more the following week
		See other SEN teachers to see if they know any other pupils who can help us with this	Mentioned it but need to remind them again
		Put cut-out patterns into file boxes	

A great deal of differentiated material is constructed by teachers themselves. The merit system is a useful way of augmenting this here. The pupils will incidentally reinforce their own learning by helping with this task.

Priority	Type	Details	Completed?
Medium	Support	*Make times tables sheets and stick on cards for Tom.* Tom is a statemented Year 10 pupil: his maths teacher says the main problem now is his basic rote number work. (Some GCSE maths tasks forbid the use of a calculator) Tom is fairly bright and his literacy has improved so he could cope with more complex work without calculators if he became more fluent. He says he'll do some work on his tables with his mother at home. I will monitor this during my 1:1 sessions with him. I could also organise for these cards to be given to other pupils who could benefit from them.	Done (individual) x3 and x4 only Will do rest over next few weeks Haven't extended it to anyone else yet

Planning for and supporting individual pupils requires careful analysis of their needs. It is often thought that innovations such as calculators make up for learning problems, but as in this case it may be necessary to promote more traditional forms of learning. Tables provide security for Tom.

Priority	Type	Details	Completed?
Medium	Support (I've only recently worked with this teacher and have done little English support)	*See P.R. Tuesday to clarify expectations re my role in the Year 10 lower middle set English class now that the statemented pupil I was there to support has been expelled from school* She still wants me to support. Sometimes I have felt my time would be better spent making materials – feel useless there about 50% of the time. Have already suggested I do models of how to quote from a poem or novel, as this seemed to present problems for many who need more explicit coaching. It could be made available as the need arose and could be combined with 1:1 guidance. She is interested but for the last two sessions has wanted me to stay in the lesson to help some pupils finish some important coursework. If I do that I have less time to make materials. I'm inclined to suggest I just do the in-class support now*.	We have now agreed I'll just do the in-class support and not the materials

*Here the mainstream teacher appears anxious to hold on to the management of the class, relegating the support teacher to a 'helping' role. Perhaps she feels that to allow the suggested course of action would reduce her autonomy: the soubriquet 'support teacher' is sometimes de-skilling for the specialist SEN teacher.

Priority	Type	Details	Completed?
Medium	Mainstream history	*Check Year 7 schemes of work for next few lessons*	Not done
Medium	Form tutor	*Check other year 10 pastoral things to do*	Rang home about a pupil Sent absence enquiries out
Low (can wait till next week)	Support (no role swaps) (Year 8 Geog. is not set)	*See Head of Geography Humanities Monday lunchtime to discuss* Geography lessons for 8 Green and 8 Blue. I won't volunteer to make any materials this week – too busy. May ask if anything required for next week. *Ask him for brief meeting to discuss my* use of grid to monitor 8 Green (numerous children with literacy difficulties) as a whole. Next week best for me. *Check if he still feels it is appropriate* for me to mainly focus on a particular individual child (with considerable learning difficulties but no statement) rather than the whole class in 8 Green. *Mention need to monitor another statemented child* in same class. (Has outgrown need for statement and needs little help but legal requirements still have to be met.) Check exam?	We spoke briefly in corridor We arranged to meet but he could not make it so I will try to talk in next lesson Not done

Every teacher will recognise this scenario. With minimal non-contact time, it is very difficult for teachers to plan together and discuss difficulties in a way which generates confidence. 'Numerous children' with literacy difficulties in one Year 8 class will present major problems for the geography teacher. The support teacher evidently feels uncomfortable about concentrating on one of them alone. She ought to have an opportunity to clarify the situation other than in a corridor. Finally, there is one last task on the list:

Priority	Type	Details	Completed?
Low	Mainstream history	*Make list of Year 7 overdue assessments and chase up*	Not done

The teacher then analyses the rationale for her decisions and priorities, and relates these to the overall functioning of the school. What is revealed is a familiar if depressing picture, of crisis management at all levels, and a general failure to realise the needs and opportunities offered by a good learning support system.

What sorts of things were done? Why?
On the whole, I tended to make sure I did tasks connected with my roles as form tutor and mainstream history teacher. Many of these are routine administrative tasks which my Head of Year or Head of History would have to come and remind me about if I did not do – I would feel naughty/guilty and that I was letting them down. Similarly, I need to make sure of my history lesson preparation and marking, otherwise there will be unpleasant consequences for me in the lesson. I often postpone picking up the exercise marking but almost always do it if I have actually taken them in. I didn't chase overdue Year 7 assessments, probably because I haven't had anyone breathing down my neck about them. Nobody but me knows they are overdue. However, within a few weeks this will become a high priority because they will be asked for soon.

Thus, the tasks completed were usually ones that I more or less had to do to keep out of trouble! They also tended to have a definite starting and finishing point – were not parts of open-ended ongoing tasks, on the whole, although I did manage to do a few pieces of work involved with ongoing learning support or curriculum development projects such as setting up the differentiated spelling pattern homework system, (designed partly to involve parents a bit more, partly to try to decrease the amount of withdrawal for extra English in the school, which causes a number of problems). However, it should be noted that I have been doing this project in fits and starts for the past year – it is gradually coming together in a form that can be used by learning support teachers other than myself. I would like to have had a whole day to devote to it; bits and pieces are not always so useful.

What sorts of things weren't done? Why?
On the whole, the learning support liaison and curriculum development work I do as a learning support teacher was the first to be dropped under pressure of time. These are actually the parts of my job that I consider the most useful in the long term. It is quite common for liaison with subject teachers I support to be continually postponed, because there are so many other pressures on teachers' time and it is probably seen as desirable but not essential, given that the learning support department in my school is only just beginning to take on a

role in curriculum development and differentiation. Subject teachers still tend to see the main function of learning support teachers as being in the class to help the children do the work set (rather than influencing the curriculum in other ways). This aspect of support work can proceed to some extent without any liaison, even though most subject teachers would agree that liaison could enhance the opportunity for the learning support teacher to make a useful contribution. Although I have a particular interest in working with different subject areas of curriculum development especially through making materials more accessible to more pupils, my present Learning-Support Coordinator and the Head of the School have not been so strongly oriented in this direction, (they are more oriented towards ensuring that statutory obligations are fulfilled, and this can mean a short term focus) so most of the materials development I have done has been my own initiative and has stemmed from my enthusiasm for this aspect of the work. My lack of training in specific learning difficulties has probably meant I was looking for some kind of unfilled niche within the SEN department. Until recently, then, my motivation to develop materials has been intrinsic. I have tended to take on a few rather large projects which took much longer to complete than I had anticipated. No one has required that I do them by a certain date. Hence, they are easy to let slip.

I sense that changes in the direction I would like to see are beginning to happen as a result of OFSTED pressure for our department to demonstrate its worth. An internal post-OFSTED review of the SEN department is being conducted by the senior staff. For the first time, they have asked to see the materials we have made during our one hour per week curriculum development time. This has resulted in more learning support staff suddenly working on materials!

I didn't plan ahead with regard to my Year 7 history lessons – I can get away with not doing that, even though I haven't taught Year 7 history before and should really be more than a couple of steps ahead of the children. Also it can mean that I don't do enough to plan for differentiation or increased balance in terms of learning activities. Perhaps I should have made this a higher priority as it would improve teaching.

What does this show about the way the school functions, especially with regard to learning support?

Support teaching and our role in curriculum development is only just beginning to be evaluated, and only as a result of comments made by OFSTED so there has been less pressure to improve this aspect of our work, and little time made available for it. Innovation and action research, while not actively discouraged, are not of high priority to senior management. INSET time for subject and support teachers to develop collaborative practices is needed but is seen as a luxury rather than a necessity by senior management. Our SEN coordinator's time is almost completely taken up with administrative matters so does not have the time available to take more of a leadership role in evaluating our current practice and developing new directions. There is a need for a better career structure for learning support teachers wishing to diversify somewhat – the coordinator has a D allowance (with an extra A for primary liaison) and the second in charge has a A. The rest of us have nothing. I've got another job (on a B) in another school for September, where hopefully I will have more scope for developing the curriculum development side of learning support. I doubt whether my colleague who is second-in-charge on an A will stay there much longer either. (A. B.)

Clearly schools have great difficulty in deciding what priority to assign to SEN in the midst of other calls on the budget. However, it is clear from the notes above that the SEN support teacher at the very least enables the smooth running of subject studies, and if the school demonstrates by its pay policy that such support is undervalued, without using INSET to help subject teachers to cope with a wide range of aptitude, the support staff may indeed vote with their feet. One thing that seems clear is that many teachers feel much happier to have the support teacher in the class, urging on slow finishers, and much less inclined to make use of her expertise in providing materials for them to use without her: it seems that this teacher's skill in designing differentiated materials is usually left untapped. This teacher has also demonstrated that some at least of her colleagues appear ambivalent about her role: in managing herself and her time she has to try to maximise her usefulness in the face of some distrust.

LEA support teachers are becoming rare. One teacher still working in this way in 1991 made a similar analysis of a week's work, and discovered that a high percentage of her time was spent on administration and not on teaching. Like other support teachers, it appears that she alone was responsible for prioritising her time. While this is unavoidable and probably desirable, it is also clear that the three headteachers for whom she worked and their staff had little idea of how to make the best use of her time and skill. She identified a number of management failures which conspired to prevent the effective use of her time:

By the time I saw the head of school 3 to remind her to tell me when she knew the Educational Psychologist was coming in, the latter had been in, on the Tuesday (the class teacher had known I was in the junior school). Why is it, the teacher has to chase EPs and Speech Therapists and never vice-versa? It makes teachers feel ignored especially when an assistant reports to me a conversation she had had with the EP about the child – although she probably needed the reassurance in what she was doing more than me. I know time is the reason and crisis management – a teacher will come to the professionals if they need guidance over an issue.

Discovered that new part-time SEN teacher is taking D out in a group for language. Class teacher and Head did not tell me; said they knew I was not in at the same time, so could not see her, so did not mention it. (Did they think I would take offence? Did they not see that the approach to reading was crucial for D and we would both need to be coordinated?) The head said 'She is appointed to teach SEN students, and we thought it would please his mother'. I arranged to come after school on Wednesday and see the new teacher. I should have seen her with the class teacher as well so that CT knew we were not undermining her. (B. B.)

This is clearly an example of 'managing upwards' in a situation where the writer is demonstrating the kinds of sensitivities which might be expected of the Head.

Another teacher working in this way describes the difficulties she experienced in engaging in the planning process with a subject teacher, and describes the process of thinking on one's feet which characterises much of the support teacher's work:

In one situation where I planned and prepared a part of the pupil's work and I knew both the long term and the short term objectives, I paced the work and could respond to the pupil's responses/progress. I understood why I had selected the chosen approaches and materials and how we would use them. I had a much fuller picture. This meant that my teaching could be more efficient and effective and I usually felt more satisfaction on completing a task.

If the work was prepared and planned by the class teacher there were times when I did not see the beginning or end of a particular piece of work. I felt with my lack of knowledge it was difficult to support the pupils effectively because I did not know what was happening.

In the instances when I was instantaneously differentiating work I felt rather like a rescue service trying to save the pupil from a sense of failure engaging in what Best (1991) calls a 'damage limitation exercise'. At the same time I was trying to gain a positive response to the situation by accessing the work set in order that something could be achieved. Such responses might not be good practice but they kept me alert and on my toes and the pupil purposefully engaged. (L. P.)

Later the same teacher identifies some of the difficulties which arose from mistrust and dislike of the support teacher's role by class and specialist teachers:

Since I am working in the rooms of class teachers, with their pupils, what happens is influenced by their attitudes towards integration of children with SEN and towards the support teacher. An example was the teacher of one class who appeared to regard teaching as a private activity (Thomas, 1993) and disliked intrusion. She was against withdrawal and did not wish to share her children. Much of my time in that class was spent watching and listening. Another example was Peter's teacher who felt he was only one in her class and she could not spend extra time discussing matters relating to him when she had others to consider. This made aspects such as collaboration, planning and evaluation difficult . . .(L. P.)

An extract from another teacher's work demonstrates the poverty of management skills within SEN departments as well as within whole schools. It is also clear that SEN expertise is not necessarily a criterion for appointment to the leadership of a SEN team:

The Head Teacher organises the timetable and therefore decides on the amount of time to be allocated to SEN. At the beginning of term I am given a timetable which indicates specific class teaching times and also blocks of time allocated to SEN. It is up to me to liaise with class teachers to agree a mutually acceptable time. There is no overall plan to allocate support time and there is no sliding scale to meet the need of the individual child. I am given the responsibility of deciding how to support a child, e.g., in class, in a group or individually. Sometimes external factors influence my decision, e.g., physical education lessons. I am also completely free to decide on the programme that I adopt, the books and games used or the lesson format. Where there is concern about a child, this will be raised at the termly review meeting, or before, if the needs are pressing. Although I have authority to organise my own timetable, group my children as I see fit and teach in my own style, I do not have any power to instigate change. On occasions I have recommended minor changes in organisation. These may or may not have been adopted, depending on the feeling of the SEN co-ordinator. Class teachers also afford me some authority as they will ask for my advice on problems of SEN management in class or on differentiation of work. As the SEN co-ordinator has no expertise in dealing with special needs, apart from her own classroom experience, her advice in this area is limited. While I feel responsible for my own teaching, I must be able to justify my actions to the SEN co-ordinator as she has overall responsibility for the delivery of special needs in the school. (C. A.)

This teacher is behaving as one might expect the SENCO herself to be acting. How will the records of support be kept and understood by the relevant staff in this case? If the child in question does proceed to a statement, such records will be vital evidence of observations and curriculum planning in the earlier stages.

 Managing the relationship with children in the context of events initiated by their parents or others but which they do not understand is another task undertaken by teachers in special schools, which cannot be described as part of the conventional curriculum. This may include medical examinations and treatment, visits to other professionals, sometimes painful manipulations, or even simply having to come to terms with not coming to school during the holidays. The teacher below describes the preparation necessary to help children with moderate learning difficulties to cope with a couple of days away from home:

Friday: Children to respite care for the weekend
 Children who spend weekends in respite care are often not told by their parents that they will be away. Time therefore needs to be spent counselling them throughout the day to emphasise that respite care is a great place to be (which it is) and not where they are sent when parents wish to punish them . . .

Respite care is provided for children whose parents need a break. Today the three children are from quite diverse backgrounds and have all reacted differently to the prospect of not being at home for the next two days (children are returned to school on Monday morning).

D., aged 9 is the eldest of five children (and the one who receives least of his parents' attention). He loves going into respite care as it is a specially indulged time for him.

J. is a Down's Syndrome child who totally 'rules the roost' at home and whose parents really need to spend time with each other and the younger child. It was that which suggested respite as they seem utterly strung out and exhausted by this mini-tyrant. How this myth that Down's Syndrome children are loving and gentle ever evolved beats me.

L. is the joker in the pack . . . He is a child whose parents appear to want him to be damaged, and who is not told until put on the school bus in the morning that he is going into respite care. He is the scapegoat of this family and is the only sibling ever sent to respite care, and quite justifiably, he feels punished and rejected.

D. reacts to respite with delight, J. with anger and L. with tearful frustration at his betrayal.

On the Monday evening when the children are bussed from school D. returns home reluctantly, J. sulks and punishes his parents by regressing to soiling and L. receives a present of his choice . . .

However, today has been spent talking about respite – where they're likely to go and visit, perhaps a film or swimming, which friends they might meet there, and of Charlie, the Respite Centre's cat. On such a day as this, children who are going into respite walk down to the shops with me and we choose for Charlie his favourite tin of Whiskas . . .

The children are picked up just that bit later than the departure of the school buses and the time seems to weigh very heavily when the building is empty. Although the staff from respite are friendly it is not difficult to tune into the children's anxieties . . .

This particularly emotionally draining end-of-week event is basically a stiff upper lip job, trying not to let the tiredness of a very hectic week impair the children's fragile confidence. Working with special needs children can be a very physically and emotionally draining experience and being the person responsible for sending two out of three reluctant children into respite care is onerous. (G. E.)

Perhaps some may say this is not teaching but social work, and teachers should not be social workers. But who will deal with such problems if they do not?

Finally, here is the list of tasks identified for the week by a teacher who is part of the senior management team for a residential special school for girls with moderate learning difficulties. At the time of writing he was IT coordinator, science coordinator, Year 9 class tutor and Head of Lower School:

The tasks:

Sort out arrangements for Lower School locker keys.

Clarify arrangements for central National Curriculum record keeping with deputy head and raise issues that will need to be addressed if Key Stage 3 SATS go ahead.

Prepare submitted Parents Handbook Curriculum Document Summaries for consideration by the Curriculum Partnership Group on Tuesday evening and chase up those not yet received.

Phone ASE to check current status of school's membership.

Read documentation relating to the implementation and recording of Key Stage 3 Science SAT pre level 3 classroom tasks.

Discuss administration of the appraisal process with the other appraiser involved in the current cycle.

Inform deputy head of possible INSET requirements in the light of recent updates to the county programme for the summer term.

Prepare reassessment report for a pupil based on notes taken at last Tuesday's full staff meeting.

Ask Head of Care to arrange an eye sight check for a Year 9 pupil following concern raised by two members of staff in recent weeks.

Organise the display of Year 11 technology work prior to this Friday's project evaluation.

Read DfE circular 16/93 'Reports on Pupils' Achievements'.

Find out Technology Coordinator's thoughts relating to the future development of technology within the school in the light of decisions reached at the recent Governors' meeting and the Education Authority's decision not to fund the new science and technology block.

Discuss alterations required in the science lab with the Head which will now be necessary following the Education Authority's decision not to fund the new science and technology block.

Begin work on the boarders' newsletter following discussion at recent senior management team meeting.

The teacher comments:

In order to ensure the effective use of my time and that of others, I often sort tasks in terms of who is involved. Out of the 14 tasks listed, 8 of them required the presence or attention of at least one other member of staff. Often the same person may be needed to accomplish a number of tasks so this also plays a part in the order in which they are dealt with. If there is an urgent and important task which needs to be addressed with a particular staff member often an additional task of lower priority will be tackled at the same time.

There are very few tasks which are dealt with simply through the passing of a memo because I am aware that most of the staff do not appreciate an endless stream of paper filling their pigeonholes. In a school where there are a number of part time staff or where, because of shift working patterns, staff are in school at different times, this method of communication does however have its place.

It is, in addition, worth noting that during the activities of a busy day a verbal request for a task to be carried out may soon be forgotten. In these circumstances a written memo may be more appropriate. An efficient way of passing on small amounts of information to all staff is through the use of the log book which is kept in the staff room. This is used to note any concerns with regard to pupils' welfare, special arrangements and general notes and reminders. Before the start of school on Monday morning I entered a note into the log to remind staff to submit any remaining curriculum document summaries for a meeting on Tuesday evening. There are actually very few tasks which I delegate as there are very few people to delegate them to. There are two support staff who do have 70 minutes non-contact time during the week and in addition there are those who find themselves under-utilised in the classroom on occasions. They may therefore make use of this time in other ways. (W. S.)

In all the examples given here, it is clear that organising and managing the tasks undertaken each week provide a foundation for what many outside fondly regard as the teacher's 'real work'. These represent actual management decisions taken by individuals working at the coal face, prioritizing their time according to the needs of the population and the other workers in the system. Managementspeak designed to describe and promote the production of widgets is not part of this world. The interface between the curriculum and the management of the teacher's 'delivery' of the curriculum is largely unaddressed in official publications. Yet it is obvious that the tasks identified here take up a significant part of a teacher's week. How much training is offered to them in time and stress management? In competition with other curricular needs, it does not command high priority.

The management and utilisation of support staff is an area of especial tension. W. S. writes:

(A) key to the effective utilization of support staff in furthering children's learning lies in the degree to which they can be used to ensure that pupils are on task and are given individual attention. One of the many dilemmas facing a teacher in a classroom is the choice that often needs to be made between maintaining high 'on task' behaviour within the group and providing individual assistance to pupils requiring clarification, prompting or correction. Thomas (1986) suggests that support staff can be used to provide a way out of this dilemma. If properly coordinated it should be possible for each member of staff to perform a particular role; one to direct the group and the other to assist individuals. Thomas refers to these roles as the activity manager and the individual helper. He also introduces a third role which he refers to as the mover whose responsibility it is to deal with resource matters and other issues which may hinder the work of the individual helper and the activity manager. Although the model is simple it provides a framework within which staff may understand the role which they are to perform and the way in which the tasks which they undertake may complement one another. In-service training directed at bringing about this way of thinking in both teaching and support staff may well prove to be highly beneficial.

Schools, by and large, are organised in Handy's phrase, as 'role cultures'. The organisation is built up in a series of

'roles or job-boxes, joined together in a logical and orderly fashion so that together they discharge the work of the organisation. The organisation is a piece of construction engineering with role piled on role and responsibility piled on responsibility. Individuals are role occupants with job descriptions that effectively lay down the requirements of the role and its boundaries. From time to time, the organisation will arrange the roles and their relationship to each other as priorities change and then reallocate the individuals to the roles.' (Handy, 1988, p. 110)

The roles in schools have proliferated in recent years: pastoral care, heads of year, subject coordinators, SENCO, but the time to fulfil those roles has not been forthcoming. It is as though mere allocation to a role will ensure its effectiveness. The other matter which is conspicuous by its absence is training. Only very recently have funded courses for curriculum coordinators become a part of the INSET scene, and SENCOs must wait until 1995–6. In the meantime the stress levels rise, and the early retirements proliferate.

3

Teachers Planning for Children

Teachers 'planning for children' includes planning the curriculum, looking at the current learning situation for the child, and initiating changes. The changing emphasis in the past few years on the curriculum rather than the child has given a new impetus to the interface between teacher, child and curriculum. Tensions arise between the concept of entitlement, and the need for flexibility based on individual needs. In any case, as Norwich (1991) points out, 'entitlement requires sufficient and appropriate staff and other resources to make it come about. When children bring different characteristics – strengths and weaknesses – to school learning, this calls for some flexibility in the selection of and balance between the common areas of learning' (p. 27).

It is easy for teachers to make assumptions about the degree to which children are aware of what they are doing in school. However, some children seem to pass their days in a hazy state of shrugged acceptance with no actual understanding of what they are doing. One support teacher (U. G.) sought to introduce self evaluation into the programme for her SEN pupils. She begins by trying to get Tim, aged 11, to think about what he has been doing:

What did you do yesterday when I wasn't there?
  (Tim thinks)
What about in the hall when you first came in?
  There was a story.
What was it about?
  I forgot.
Did you do anything else?
  We sung first I think.
What did you sing?
  No, I forgot. I keep forgetting what I do.
. . .

Have you done a lot this morning?
  Yeah.
What did you think of your work?
  All right.

Did you do good work?
  Yeah.
What was the best bit?
  That (points to a model he made yesterday).
What do you think about your maths?
  All right.
What do you think about getting it all right?
  All right.
  . . .

What did you think of it? (a computer programme)
  It was quite silly. Rubbish. (Thinks) A little bit rubbish. You can't go nowhere.
  (Tim kept choosing options which came to a dead end.)
If we had found the frog, would it have been silly?
  No.
Would you have another go to find the frog?
  Yep.
What did you learn? (about how to start)
  T (he tries to spell TAKE but got no further)
  One day you can remember but the next day you can't.

The responses in these conversations with Tim are typical. Often he has difficulty in remembering what has happened or even what has gone before. He appears to have few personal opinions, usually going along with the group around him. Tim finds it difficult to make choices or decisions so his statements are often non-committal or indecisive in their nature. If asked to make a judgement about anything his usual reply is 'OK' or to go along with the majority. When it comes to his own work or achievements, Tim's response is usually either to shrug his shoulders, an 'OK' or an embarrassed smile. However, if it is a piece of work which is obviously wrong, say in maths, he will admit it is 'no good'. With this background self evaluation for Tim presents difficulties associated with his limited self expression and poor memory. The relevance of these difficulties depends on the context within which the self evaluation is being used and the reason for using it. However I do use the process with Tim and we have developed a chart for his immediate response to work just done. On the chart he gives himself credits for work completed and standard achieved, working towards a target total each week. This chart has also helped with another difficulty – Tim used never to finish anything.

The following extract shows how a teacher working in a school for children with severe learning difficulties uses systematic observation and assessment of a child with profound and multiple learning difficulties to inform her individual programme planning:

As J. was new to the school it was vital that as much information as possible should be gathered about the child's strengths and needs. After discussion with colleagues and J.'s parents it was decided that the assessment procedure should begin with observation of J. Everyone agreed that a general picture needed to be painted of the child. School staff observed J. in a variety of situations, noting J.'s actions, sounds and responses to the classroom environment. A meeting was arranged with J.'s parents to discuss these observations and use the parents' knowledge of the child in naturalistic settings to formulate the following strengths and needs list.

Strengths	Needs
Has head control	
Can visually track objects	To develop visual/ auditory skills
Can visually fixate on objects	To explore/ become more aware of her environment
Enjoys adult attention	
Likes being held and talked to	To develop motor control
Laughs when happy and content	To express preferences
Likes music and singing	To signal for 'more' of something, i.e., tangibles and human contact
Enjoys dinner time	
Uses voice to attract attention	To become aware of cause and effect
Can show discomfort or distress by crying	

From initial observation and consultation with parents about the child's strengths and needs, the teacher then began to use more systematic assessment tools to guide programme planning:

From the meeting with parents, it was agreed that developing J.'s communication should become a priority. Intervention observation was to be carried out to gain baseline information about J.'s existing communicative abilities. These observations involved investigative procedures; setting up contexts and watching what J. would do; hypothesis testing, i.e., asking 'what happens if?' questions, e.g., if the person feeding ceased to give J. much attention, and instead diverted her attention to a child sitting next to J., what would J. do? Would she, and how would she try to redirect the adult's attention from the other child to herself?

In addition to these investigative procedures, the teacher also used commercial tools in her assessment.

The Preverbal Communication Schedule (Kiernan and Reid, 1987) was used to help observe, assess and record J.'s 'informal communicative behaviours', including 'communication through looking', 'expression of emotion' and 'communicative use of sounds' (Kiernan and Reid, op. cit.). 'Sequential sampling' (McBrien, Farrell, Foxen, 1992) was used to gather more detailed information about the things that J. liked and disliked. For example, J. was presented with a variety of toys and her reactions to them were recorded, to discover her preferences and to see if J. could indicate that she wanted 'more' time playing with some toys and not others.

From this information, the teacher devised the following flow diagram representing long- and short-term aims for J. in communication.

Long term aims:
(a) for J. to express her needs and interests and bring about change,
(b) to make sense of her immediate environment,
(c) to influence the behaviour of people in her environment.

Short term aims:

Social/emotional Development	Environmental Awareness	Formal Communication	Motor Development
Collaborative play routines	Cause and effect	Signal for 'more'	Use of trolley board for mobility
	Switch toys; Single switch computer games	Object symbols	

From long- and short-term aims, the teacher (J. K.) is able to devise teaching programmes in different curricular areas. The lesson plan below represents a small component of a teacher's 'motor sensory' programme offering a child with PMLD experience of 'cause and effect' (C. M.):

Tommy: Sensory motor programme (cause and effect)
    Intention: to encourage T. to use his feet and hands to activate a single switch controlling various switch toys.
    Equipment: Moving pig, police car, dog and frog up a tree.
    Situation: (a) using foot – sit T. on a bench with an adult behind to support/prompt/reward. Place toy to T.'s right-hand side and fix switch next to T.'s right foot. Adult should be in a position to lean forward to activate the switch (prompt) and offer verbal, physical and facial encouragement/reward.
    (b) using hand – place T. in his standing frame with the toy and switch to the right-hand side of his tray. Fix switch firmly near his right hand. Stand to one side of T. so he can see your face. Give verbal, physical and facial encouragement/reward.
    Method: Show T. what to do by activating the toys for the first 3 times. Using strong facial expression and intonation of voice. Encourage T. to activate toys using physical prompts if necessary. Praise him immediately when he activates the toy. Use the attached recording schedule to record T.'s performance. (C. M.)

Observation as the foundation for curriculum planning is also demonstrated in the following extract: an account of a support teacher's involvement with an ESL (English as a second language) pupil:

I took the opportunity to observe Sebastian in the classroom where there was no support provision. During a thirty minute period I focused on his interaction with other pupils. The teacher had previously discussed the topic being studied and outlined the task set. Sebastian shared a table with three other boys, one of whom was a fellow Pole and a support for him. He had his back to the teacher and never reacted to any of the questions asked, or instructions given – possibly disinterested, but more likely not understanding anything which was being said. Sebastian occasionally spoke in Polish to his classmate. His communication with other boys was made through eye contact and gestures. He did not attempt to speak any English, or show interest in the conversation or activities of his neighbours. He pretended to work by taking a very long time to copy headings and draw a table. He did not attempt to complete any of the written exercises set. On a second occasion I was similarly concerned about his lack of interaction with either staff, or students. I therefore targetted his periods of silence and used duration recording techniques in order to monitor the results. During a seventy minute lesson Sebastian spoke only once, to me, asking me to explain the teacher's instuctions. On one occasion he played with droplets of water dripping from the taps above the sink, smiling and laughing quietly with his ESL (and non-Polish speaking) neighbour. Both observations were cause for concern. Although a two month period had elapsed since the first occasion some things remained unchanged. On neither occasion did Sebastian directly interact with his classroom teacher. (He did make some small contact with me, when he possibly saw me as the person paid to help him.) His communication with fellow pupils was still limited to actions and gestures, rather than linguistically based. He attempted some form of work in both lessons, but only exercises which required him to copy information. He did not attempt any original work of his own. It is interesting to note that at this stage his fellow Pole was no longer sitting beside Sebastian, but was attempting to present himself as an independent learner no longer in need of support and he therefore disassociated himself from Sebastian, who no longer benefited from his help. The three other stage one ESL pupils were now speaking English, although their motivation and skills in written English were not as good as the other Polish student's. Quite obviously Sebastian's progress was slow. It is also interesting to note that his attendance record was not as good as the other ESL pupils, often an indication of an unhappy student.

Whilst commenting on the conduct of the student it is also important to focus on the conduct of the teachers. The issue of the placement by the authority of stage one ESL students in mainstream classes was much debated by the staff at the school. There was particularly strong feeling that the students should receive some basic support at a reception centre prior to entering schools.

Once the student was in the classroom he should receive individual support; almost a translatory service. The problem was viewed as an LEA one which should be resolved by the LEA and not by the ordinary classroom teacher. Most staff felt there was little they could do for the ESL pupil. No one had any specialist training in this area or felt they had the time to produce individual materials designed for use by the pupils. The staff were not unsympathetic to these students, the boys were welcomed, and liked, but staff did feel that the LEA could do something to help.

As Special Needs (and unofficially ESL) co-ordinator I decided to focus my support programme on Sebastian's English, mathematics and science lessons. In other areas of the curriculum where Sebastian was receiving support I hoped that any kind of help was better than nothing.

In mathematics Sebastian had been placed in the top set where he would receive help from his fellow Pole. He appeared to have difficulty coping with the work so it was decided to place him in the bottom set which needed no written explanation and were straightforward additions, subtractions, multiplications and divisions. This was one of the very few occasions in Sebastian's time at the school when he functioned as an independent learner. He worked quickly and appeared keen to please. When I set him new exercises he smiled broadly and said 'is easy'. At this stage he sat alone not really communicating with fellow students, but as time passed he sat with other students. He had now proved his ability with basic mathematics and was placed on an SMP course selected for its readability and appropriate vocabulary. It was hoped that in using his skills and understanding in mathematics he might also develop his linguistic skills. Sebastian always brings his books to the lesson and rarely asks for help. Work takes place on an individual basis and Sebastian has already gone further than his native English speaking classmates. In the class examination in March he gained 79%. It is hoped that as time goes by Sebastian will make progress with his English and in mathematics and will have the opportunity to move into other sets more appropriate to his ability. (H. A.)

Another support teacher uses her knowledge of the child and the information he gives her to enhance the teaching of spelling. This extract demonstrates how simplistic some of the arguments about spelling can be. Creativity is part of the teacher's armoury:

A.'s class teacher had expressed her concern about his spelling. We discussed this between us and after approaching the parents for their agreement I did some assessments with him. To establish a base line I tested him on the Daniels and Diack spelling test, this gave him a spelling age of 7y 8m which was 1y 9m below his chronological age. I went over the words of the test with A. and asked him if he could tell which ones were wrong. While we were talking through the words he gave me some clues about his problems e.g. he said he was not sure when to put an 'e' on the end of a word. I also looked through his books to see if there were any clues in his work as to which words were most common. After that I then went through the sounds with him – first dictating them and then asking him to read them. He managed all the single sounds apart from 'y' and 'u' which he muddled. I had also given him some common words to spell – said (sied) they (thay) and the days of the week. He managed to spell most of these except Tuesday (Tusday), Thursday (Thrsday) and Saturday (Satday). He was not sure what to write for the 'ur' in Saturday. He knew that 'er' made the sound but didn't think it was the right one. He also knew how to spell Wednesday because his father had suggested to him that he should pronounce it Wed-nes-day. As a start on helping him I pointed out the three ways of making the sound 'ur' and showed him that it was the same one in Thursday and Saturday. I also suggested that he thought of Tuesday as Tu-es-day to help him to remember to write in the 'e' – then worked on the letter groups 'ight' and 'ould'. I gave him some mnemonics to help him with these 'I go home tonight' and 'oh you little duck'. I asked him how he learnt his spellings and suggested that as well as 'look, cover, write and check' he needed to say the letters as well – pointing to them as he said them and trying to say them with his eyes shut. I followed this up with weekly sessions in a small group of children with similar problems and I tried to encourage the children to use their joined up writing to help them with their spellings. Many of them were unsure about writing 'b' and 'd' correctly so we worked on this using various multi-sensory techniques. A. had said that he had problems knowing when to put an 'e' on the end of a word. I went over the vowels with the group – names and sounds and played games and computer games concentrating on the silent 'e'. I went right back to the beginning to ensure that they could spell and write two letter words correctly and we are now building on these skills. I am also getting them to practise sounding out a word before they attempt to write it down. All the members of the group seem somewhat uncertain of the consonant blends so I will work on those as well. At the moment it is too early to assess formally whether there has been any improvement in A.'s spelling age, but he himself says that he feels more confident and he is remembering the rules that we have gone over. (L. G.)

Planning the micro-curriculum in this way is a component of the overview which teachers must have of the whole child and his placement. Often, most often, the teacher has little say in the overall management of a pupil's school career. However, in the initiation of a statement or a review, there is an opportunity and a responsibility to direct change. Teachers in special schools are accustomed to the seemingly arbitrary assignment of new pupils to their classes. Sometimes this is not accompanied by adequate information, and the child may encounter fresh difficulties in the new school. The decision to seek yet another change is not taken lightly. This teacher is working in a school for children with moderate learning difficulties and has made the decision to refer one of her pupils for reassessment. She hopes that this will result in a new placement in a school where his violent, unpredictable behaviour can be contained. However, this is easier said than done:

Perhaps the mistakes concerning S.'s admission to the school were the culmination of (his mother's) determination to 'do the right thing' for her child, the casual suggested placement and acceptance by the authority and school, but the real issue, that of S.'s bewilderment at his new surroundings and routines, were only really put in their true perspective when the report from his former school indicated that S. had followed a behaviour modification programme. No real surprises then that without the continuation of this programme, (whether you are for or against behaviour modification) that educationally and socially, S. began a decline that I fear will be irreversible unless his new placement is established quite quickly. The report from his previous school accurately identifies S.'s autistic features, his violence, his speech impairment and his inability to interact with his peers. Predictably there is now a whole new list of behaviours to add, which include: running away; not responding to adult instruction; becoming increasingly unaware of his own safety and that of others; becoming sexually demonstrative and obsessive towards children and adults of both sexes; hitting out indiscriminately and, increasingly hitting himself; only responding to physical threats (recently the deputy head phoned S.'s mother and requested that he be taken home as his level of violence could not be contained. The mother was livid and demanded to know why as a man, the deputy had not given S. a 'bloody good hiding'.) S.'s mother singled out S.'s class teacher as being actively racist towards her son and was as the children say 'gobsmacked' when told that the teacher had five mixed race children of her own. It wasn't just factors such as the rapidly rising roll, the new head coming to grips with the demands of an ailing school or the changes in personnel but that certain key agencies like the educational social worker and the educational psychologist were for a variety of reasons not permanently assigned to the school. Even when the mother came to terms with S. either being excluded from school on a more frequent basis or being reassessed with a view to a more appropriate educational placement, the mother was reluctant and insisted that she be accompanied by her sister who was an educational psychologist. A gathering mountain of behavioural forms have accumulated since the decision that S. really is not benefiting from what the school has to offer and that as numbers increase, his personal space decreases and he shows more and more that he is regressing. S. has had a speech therapy input throughout his time with us. The speech therapist reports that overall there is very little change in his command of language or his concentration span although a few tiny steps have been taken – the same sentiments that all staff feel – but this educational improvement, however slight, does not make up for the mercurial physical violence that S. so frighteningly displays. It wasn't until the last six months that all agencies involved with S. really began working towards his reassessment with a view to finding a new school – a more appropriate establishment that meets the autistic needs that S. displays. Retrospectively it seems as though the child was condemned to two and a half years hard labour before any constructive action was taken, but it has only been since the onset of puberty, when S. has become uncontainable and has actually regressed and become unhappy, that any progress has been made in reviewing his placement. Once the decision to reassess S.'s needs was given high priority, much time has been given to finding a suitable school that would provide a setting where S. could continue to make, albeit small, educational and social steps forward. Inevitably this has not been an easy task as autistic schools are justifiably reluctant to take on a pupil with such a record of increasingly violent behaviour. Autistic children do not usually manifest such high levels of physical and overtly sexual behaviours – which basically means that even though S.'s papers have gone to the Panel, and a new placement has been actively sought, two schools have made it quite clear that S. would not be accepted – basically because he needs a ratio of one-to-one and schools (especially with the introduction of LMSS) cannot provide this.

Basically, the agreed course of action though confirmed by a whole plethora of professionals, cannot be implemented until a school within the catchment area has firstly been approved by S.'s mother and that that school or unit is prepared to accept him. In conclusion; there is no conclusion . . . despite the best will in the world it is going to be very difficult to find the correct placement for this child. I predict that S. will shortly direct his anger towards his mother (if he hasn't already) and she in turn will request a statement for boarding . . . that is the reality. However in the interim – for a very long time, S. will continue his education with us, until he is permanently excluded for violence towards either pupils or staff. (G. E.)

A peripatetic teacher of the visually impaired describes how her planning involves a range of personnel in the school in a delicate exchange of information and skill. The peripatetic teacher is always in a difficult position; she may have a wide range of difficulties to deal with, but the nature of her job means that she will rarely have time to actually execute the plans she makes, and may be criticised by school staff if they do not understand or sympathise with her ideas. She describes some plans for children in different schools:

The primary school I am visiting on Tuesday morning has not had a visually impaired child before, so it is my first visit. I will no longer be just a name or a service in that school, but a person. Initial visits are very important in setting up the pattern for future ones. I have found that a successful initial introduction to the school often secures good liaison in the future. One of my aims is to introduce myself to the key people in the school i.e. the head, the SENCO, the class teacher, the support teacher, the Special Needs Assistant and, of course, the child. Hopefully, these people will all know of my visit and be expecting me. Sometimes internal communication within the school breaks down and the head does not tell the class teacher of my appointment. This is not a good way to start a relationship, but is out of my control to a certain extent. (I always check that the head is going to tell the class teacher about the time and date of my visit, and make sure that I know the names of the key people.) I will also meet the other children in the class and perhaps get an idea of the ethos within the classroom and how the class as a whole is functioning.

Thomas and Feiler's (1988) view of integration is that:

'The closed door of the traditional classroom will have to be opened to let in other adults: classroom assistants, support teachers, parents and visiting professionals. If this is mismanaged, the classroom will become a disorganised muddle, where the class teacher views such other adults as intruders. But, if managed well, the classroom can become a place where a rich variety of well-planned teaching strategies can be implemented so that all the children benefit.'

I have experienced the feeling of being an 'intruder' and believe that much depends on the personality and self-esteem of the class teacher as well as on my approach.

Providing there is time I hope to have discussions with the above mentioned members of staff either separately or together and to give out information on: the visual condition of the child – both generally and specifically; the implications within the classroom; some materials for use with the child e.g. heavy-lined exercise books, black felt pens, large print calculator. The discussions will centre around the child's history and developmental progress through to ways of differentiating materials for access to the National Curriculum.

During the above session I hope to have given time for the teachers and the SNA to air their anxieties and difficulties. I will try to listen well in a non judgemental way and to be encouraging about things that are going well. At the very least I will have given respectful attention but I hope to have helped lead the way to some solutions or given ideas and made suggestions for trying different approaches/methods.

One of my most important functions is to observe the visually impaired child and spend some time talking to her about her vision and how she feels she is coping – what she enjoys doing and what is difficult. Sometimes this is the first time the child's vision has been given direct attention and, as such, can be quite revealing about the child's self-image.

I will also be attending an Annual Review of a Year 6 child whose parents are very anxious about secondary transfer. In this meeting I hope to be able to allay their fears by suggesting a programme of introduction to the secondary school for her support teacher to follow towards the end of term. This will consist of planning the child's journey to school and giving her the chance to experience it with and without help. Spending more time in the secondary school, finding out the layout of the various classrooms, and practising the negotiation of stairways could be helpful. I am also going to suggest a formal referral to the Borough's Social Service department which deals with visual impairment so that the child can have a full assessment of her mobility and independence needs. My other main goal at this review meeting is to ensure that the child's support continues, at least for the first term, into the secondary school. I think it is going to be a very challenging time for the child and do not want her self-confidence to be diminished by withdrawing the support too soon. Another review at the end of the child's first term would be ideal.

On Friday when I visit one of my secondary schools I hope to make a short video of A., a fourteen year old partially sighted boy, using an electronic reading aid. I have borrowed the aid from the company on a trial basis to see if it is beneficial in speeding up A.'s reading.

CONCLUSION

All of the above extracts are taken from work carried out before the Code of Practice (DfE, 1994) laid down the duties of the SEN Coordinator. They are, however, good examples of the range of tasks which are expected in relation to the children for whom an Individual Education Plan is contemplated. They involve not only the SENCO herself, but also class teachers and specialist advisory teachers. It remains to be seen whether adequate time is to be set aside for the completion of these tasks.

4

Teachers Working with Parents and Others

Bastiani (1987) proposed four basic modes of interaction between parents and professionals, which reflected the kinds of relationship chosen by teachers and other professionals as appropriate. These were compensation, communication, accountability and partnership. When these models are presented to teachers they usually respond that all are part of the relationship at some time but that they strive towards partnership as an ideal. However, in 1993, Bastiani suggested that although everyone is in favour of partnership there is a 'conspiracy to avoid looking at it too critically in case it falls apart . . . perhaps it is more helpful to see partnership as a process, a stage in a process or something to work towards rather than something that is a fixed state or readily achievable' (p. 113).

Again teachers themselves find it hard to actually define partnership, and sometimes find it difficult to reconcile the joint action implied in the term with the accountability underlined by recent legislation. The Code of Practice (1994) attempts to put flesh on the bones of partnership and urges schools to recognise the 'unique knowledge and information' which parents have. 'Professional help can seldom be effective unless it builds upon parents' capacity to be involved, and unless parents consider that professionals take account of what they say and treat their views and anxieties as intrinsically important' (DfE, 1994, para. 2.28).

Annual reviews, and formal parents' evenings sometimes appear to militate against good models of partnership:

The organisation regarding SEN pupils is unsatisfactory for both parents and staff, and when each Parents Evening comes round minor organisational changes are made. The basic format is that once a term a letter is sent home inviting parents to choose a time to see the class teacher. At the end of the letter there is a sentence requesting the parents to see the SEN teacher, where appropriate. When the classroom times are negotiated between class teachers, then the support teachers try to fit parents in, so as to avoid an overlap. On the evening all teachers take longer than anticipated and as a result the support teachers frequently have to search out parents who have been delayed elsewhere. All class teachers have a private meeting place. Here they cannot be overheard. All five support teachers are based in a noisy central atrium where unsupervised children congregate and where parents meet and pass through on their way from one class to another. The noise level is quite high and the area is not distraction-free for either teachers or parents, so it is difficult to concentrate and discuss delicate or worrying matters. The policy of the school is not to have children present at these interviews. Parents to whom I have spoken find it difficult to see several class and support teachers on the same evening. Although class and support teachers do communicate before such an event, occasionally conflicting reports are given to the parents. There is also a great pressure of time. A 'normal' interview is timed to last for five minutes. When a parent has anxieties and questions, this does not give much time for an exchange of ideas. (C. A.)

In this chapter we include some examples which reflect SEN teachers' experiences of partnership on the ground. Some of these are positive, others less so; all require tact, knowledge and self-confidence.

One important point is that the SEN teachers' interactions with parents must be seen in the context of an ongoing concern in which a child's needs are the focus of discussion with other teachers and perhaps other professionals. The SEN teacher, however, is often the one who has the task of discussing all these issues with parents.

The following describes the actions taken by one teacher (M. J.) in a primary school, in respect of two statemented children in her class. She first lists the actions and then discusses the issues arising from them.

Case 1 – K
Tuesday:
1. Discuss progress of K. with teacher assistant, in terms of social, intellectual and physical development. Make notes and add to profile.
2. Meet with SEN coordinator to discuss:
    i.   short-term and long-term timetable for K.
    ii. where will K. go next year (move up with rest of class/stay in reception/ Special Unit at X school)
    iii. what records should I be keeping in relation to K.'s on-going assessment?

Wednesday:
3. Talk to teacher assistant about progress of K. Both of us think she has improved in terms of physical strength and confidence. We feel that our primary goal of increased socialisation with other class members, needed after continual absenteeism due to illness, is working well and that her language skills are improving, as hoped, because of this. We discuss our next main objectives and how we will attempt to accomplish these. These are then recorded using the school's six weekly plan. Discuss with teacher assistant new targets for K.
4. Observe K.'s interaction with other children. Has her interaction improved as a result of the programme of activities carried out by the teacher assistant and myself?

5. Formal meeting to be arranged with K.'s parents, SEN coordinator, Headteacher, and myself. Informal chat with K.'s mum: offer of moral support and discussion of K.'s progress.

At 3.30 pm: I spoke to K.'s mum about progress. I was able to tell her of good progress as a result of teacher assistant being employed (lhr 30 mins. each day) because of statement. Mum agreed with me and is pleased with improvement. Mum still concerned that the possibility of extended absenteeism might hamper progress. Reminded her to provide dates so that a meeting can be arranged between parents, myself, the school's coordinator, and the headteacher.

Friday:
I speak with SEN coordinator at 12.00 noon to arrange meeting about K.'s progress and to discuss new target setting. She has said she will 'get back to me on it' but I shall chase up and make sure I have a date for next week.

Case 2 – A
Tuesday:
1. Talk to mum as follow up to A.'s visit to hearing unit. At 10.30am: A.'s mum drops him into class after visit to hearing unit. Mum obviously upset and tearful. Asked NNEB to mind class whilst I take A.'s mum to private group room. Mum explains that A. will need a hearing aid and is shocked by this. After comforting mother, I suggest that we make a definite appointment to meet after school next week to discuss how A. is coping with the hearing aid.
2. 1.20pm: Hearing specialist arrives at school to meet me and see A. in school setting, and to show me and NNEBs how to insert and check hearing aid. Explains that she is quite willing to talk to class about the hearing unit and about the hearing aid. Manage to talk to her briefly about ways I can help A. and to make myself clear and easier to lip read. She also explains about A.'s condition and problems that A. might face with sudden hearing enrichment. We arrange a time for her to re-visit class next week.

Wednesday:
8.55am: Reassured A.'s mum that first day went without problems. Also that hearing specialist has come into school and has talked to class and staff in Early Years Unit.

Friday:
2.00pm: Meet with SEN coordinator and again asked her for a meeting date.
2.30pm: Speak to NNEBs about establishing routine for administering inhalers, putting in A.'s hearing aid and checking on K.'s general health status.
3.30pm: Speak to both K.'s and A.'s mothers informally, about how children are coping in class.

Still to do:
Meeting with SEN coordinator.
Detailed observation of K.

Check on date for formal meeting with K.'s parents, SEN coordinator etc.
Make notes on A. for consultation with his mum next week.
Share target setting and results with K.'s mum.

I felt that actually listing and prioritising what I needed to do, and have done this week helped in identifying a real area of concern – the problem of not being able to pin down the SEN coordinator for long enough to make an appointment. I found this frustrating as there are many matters that I need to discuss with her. I also found that there was no central place that I could find information about this for myself. I intend to take my diary to her classroom next week and fix a series of dates with her. I found that planning meeting times between me and the teacher assistant and for the NNEBs extremely useful, and was able to use their comments in my own record-keeping for both A. and K. As these meetings can only take place when I am free from contact with the children, this has resulted in sacrificing my playtimes. However, I felt that this was a management decision I was prepared to take as it would otherwise entail asking the teacher assistant to stay over her contracted time, which I feel would be unfair to her. I found that there was a greater need for my role and the SEN coordinator to be examined in school, for as Wolfendale (1989) states, implicit in the effective functioning of all those involved in primary teaching, there are some fundamental features:

'that the actors, for example teachers, parents, support personnel, governors, roles, functions, and responsibilities have been properly defined, clarified and delineated so that they are comfortable with them; that the relationships between and among these principal actors have actually been delineated and made explicit, so that when it comes to the exercising of role and responsibilities to do with the special needs provision – their demarcations facilitate the application of policy.' (Wolfendale, 1989) (M. J.)

Another teacher engages with the children in discussion of their problems and follows this up with talking to parents. This teacher appears to espouse a definite partnership with parents, and sees her task as engendering and fostering positive reinforcement for parents as well as children:

A problem surfaced last week with a Year Five boy. Briefly the background to this was that he had received SEN help in Year Three and had made good progress. Therefore he received no SEN support last year. He has been experiencing difficulties with basic literacy skills and rejoined his Year Five group with diminishing motivation. I had discussed this with him in the (withdrawal) group, and also with his class teacher who commented that he worked hard in class. I suggested she talked with M. and as I was testing individual children that afternoon, I would find some time to talk with him too. He and I had an open and honest discussion as to how he felt, what he wanted to achieve and how he thought he could best do this. I asked if he objected to our discussing this with the group to see how they felt, and told him how brave I thought he had been to talk about his difficulties, and I suggested he told his parents. His reply was that mum already knew.

This week I need to continue close regular liaison with his class teacher to monitor his attitude, motivation, progress and general happiness. I also need to talk with his mother to get her perspectives on M.'s learning and motivation. I will also discuss with the group of Year Five children M.'s concerns about the curriculum and the teaching/learning approach and encourage M. to lead the discussion putting his suggestions forward, which is to concentrate on story-writing.

When working with J. who has a statement I will continue the teaching of basic literacy skills and he can plan the order of this work, which he knows must be done every lesson we have, and includes reading, and comprehension work, flashcards and phonics, initial consonant blends and vowel digraphs . . .

What I want to achieve with J. is ongoing. My long term goals are for improved positive interaction with adults and peers, being relaxed, happy, pleasant and openly communicative. I want to encourage flexibility of routine so that he will accept changes more readily. I want him to appreciate his own efforts and what he achieves, and be pleased with this because he has tried so hard. I am encouraging him to express his emotions and to do so in more appropriate ways. I am working for him to accept things as they are and to take positive steps to improve them, empowering him to make decisions knowing that he can affect things positively.

I would like to see J.'s mum on Thursday when she picks him up from school to have an informal chat. I want to reassure her about the positive changes in his attitude, motivation and progress. I want J. to be present because I think they will both benefit from mutual respect.

I met M.'s and J.'s mothers on separate occasions. M.'s mother was very supportive of him and very proud of the way he responded to his difficulties. I told her succinctly of our philosophy. I informed her of the change in SENs in the withdrawal group and how I envisaged M.'s progress with skills and concepts which would continue but in a different way. I reassured her that M. would in the ordinary class be able to continue the individual programme of work set up by his class teacher, and would continue to work with motivation in class. Mum was very pleased that he was receiving support in school and was willing to help him at home. Mum, as well as M. himself, has become increasingly anxious over the last three terms about his progress, and I feel I need frequent, regular informal contact with her so that she can see M.'s progress and keep his learning in perspective.

Interestingly when I talked with J.'s mum, whilst he was present, she seemed embarrassed and somewhat surprised when I told her that J. thought she had brilliant ideas for stories. I told her how pleased I was with J., his atttitudes and progress, and that she must be very proud of him. I know the background and that his mother wrote a very vivid and moving letter to the educational psychologist for J.'s statement. With other personal difficulties in the family I appreciate the need for honesty and positive communication. (N.B.)

Not all relationships between parents and schools are positive: and sometimes the process of identification and assessment is a painful one:

I recently had an interview with a foster parent of a pupil in my class. The pupil – B. – has profound and multiple learning difficulties and has been statemented. The parent had been sent a copy of B.'s Individual Educational Plan (IEP) beforehand. I discussed the IEP, elaborating on some areas, explaining in detail how aspects of the IEP are taught and for what reason. The parent did not ask me any questions but was happy to respond when I questioned her about B. and asked for advice (particularly with regards to feeding). The parent's attitude was one of caution and wariness. The background to this interview is very significant – the parent is fighting B.'s statement. She wants a one-to-one for B. The Borough's response has been to address each individual point on the statement (the whole of which provided the basis for the demand for one-to-one support for B.). Effectively the borough has seen to it that all demands have been met by the school and as such has avoided having to confront the one-to-one issue itself, because the reasons for this are no longer under contention. The result of this is that the only way the parent can force her case is by discrediting the school. She needs to prove that we are not meeting B.'s needs and as such she should be given a one-to-one. There was definitely an element of embarrassment during the interview but she was determined to fight. The parent does know that B. is cared for and educated at school but it is detrimental to her overall fight to admit this. The parent is very clear that B. has a right to the very best education and that it is the school's responsibility to provide this – I think her experiences with the statementing procedure have tainted her attitude towards the school and education in general. I am sure that she does not have complete confidence in us. To a limited degree the parent has absorbed the 'moral model', in that she sees it as her duty, almost a crusade, to give B. every educational advantage and the opportunity to get the best out of life. I say to a limited degree because the parent is not trying to make B. perfect but get what she thinks B. is entitled to. She adheres more strongly to a child centred model. She is optimistic about B.'s abilities and her potential to progress educationally (but is also realistic). B. is lucky to have someone so strong and articulate to fight for her needs. Obviously the situation is different for the school and the trust in the relationship with the parent has been destroyed – However I cannot help admiring her motives and determination. (O. J.)

P. arrived at infant school with a statement of special educational need. His Fragile X condition had been diagnosed early and he had been attending the workplace nursery at the local hospital where he had regularly seen the speech and language therapist. He was experiencing all the usual difficulties of a child having this condition. His mother was very pleased to have secured a place for him at the local school. The grandparents lived with the family and mother worked full time so grandfather, who seemed a very old, gentle man, was P.'s main carer during the day.

Unfortunately the reception classroom was a rather cramped and crowded hut in a small concrete playground – This seemed hardly ideal for the physical needs of P. but he settled very well with the help of his daily (2 hours) assistant.

After two terms the review was held. Socially P. had become more confident, independent and rather more assertive at saying 'no' to tasks designed for him. He hovered on the edge of most class activities. His fine pinch-grip had not improved, so holding anything, especially a pencil, was difficult. Left/right coordination showed very little improvement but some progress with hand/eye coordination had been made.

At the review the teacher (an NQT) and the Occupational Therapist felt that P.'s physical programme was not being implemented fully due to lack of resources, time and the size of the mainstream class. The options before the review panel were: (a) repeat the reception year. (b) join his peers in year one. (c) placement in special school. P.'s mother wished him to remain at the school. She believed that her son had a medical condition from which he would ultimately get better. She believed this so strongly that she had not shared all the medical facts with the grandparents who spent a great deal of time with him. It is interesting to note that the classroom assistant felt grandfather shared some of P.'s physical characteristics and movements.

The general feeling of the multi-professional panel was that P.'s needs were not being properly met in the present situation. Mother reluctantly agreed to consider the possibility of placement at special school. Her revision of the temporary 'medical model' she had previously accepted was made more difficult by her reluctance to share all the facts with her family. While a baby and toddler there had not seemed a great difference between P. and his peers. Diagnosis of Fragile X had been early and she had received a good level of support from her GP and the authority. She had felt optimistic that P. would 'get better'.

P.'s mother now began to see the physical and verbal ability gap widening and her son's frustration and disruption in the classroom. After several further discussions with the E.P. she agreed to a transfer to a local special school. P's mother ultimately felt that the professionals knew what was best for her son. I believe that most of the multi-professional panel concerned in the case felt uncomfortable in trying to persuade the mother to consider the special school option but believed it was the correct course for P. at the time. (P. D.)

Sometimes the failures in communication are on both sides:

S. is in the Reception class and her mum has been having difficulty getting her to come in to school. I became involved when Mrs M. came in to school to ask for help and the Deputy Head passed her on to me. On Monday I met S. at the gate and took her from her mum. She cried a little but was soon comforted and chatted easily. I telephoned Mrs M. to reassure her that S. was all right and to plan a strategy for the week. We agreed that the Nursery Nurse would meet S. every day. However Mrs M. did not keep to the plan and this prompted the Deputy Head to write a letter to the parents to request their cooperation, at which they were offended. Further meetings plans were arranged and gradually S. was persuaded to come into school with her sister and was able to stand up at a recent birthday assembly and say that she was getting better at coming in to school by herself. There are several points to note in this situation. Firstly there were too many people involved. The parents needed to have one line of contact identified. Secondly, and as a result of numbers involved, lines of communication were not absolutely clear and issues became confused. Thirdly it was unfortunate that Mrs M. was unable to abide by our arrangement. If we had managed the first day we may have progressed successfully. Lastly since we know that S. is happy in school we have to remember that we may be dealing with the 'needs' of the parent rather than the child. Also that we do not see the child at home and we have to take into account the parents viewpoint. Solity and Raybould (1988) suggest that 'Schools have to work towards establishing a positive relationship with parents in an atmosphere of mutual trust and acceptance . . . both parties can be seen to have different interests and concerns'. This relationship is in danger when parents are feeling anxious about their child, especially so if they perceive that the school is apportioning blame to them. (V. Q.)

But sometimes there is a positive outcome to a difficult situation:

This interview was arranged between the parents of a child in my class and my head teacher for 9.30am and I was to be available from 10.00–10.30 whilst my class was with another teacher. The interview was asked for by the parents and it followed a psychological report on the child. The report had been suggested by the headteacher and paid for by the parents. They would obviously want to discuss the next steps to be taken and be clear about the school's role. I called at the office at 10.00 and was immediately invited into the headteacher's study. The parents are professional people and older than most of our parents, with only the one child. There had been an emotional discussion before my arrival because the test results had shown Jane not only as having many dyslexic tendencies, but also as having quite a low IQ, although there were many positive pointers and helpful recommendations in the report. The low IQ was quite a shock for the parents and difficult for them to accept. The mother said it had made them feel like giving up, implying that nothing could change this. She was applying an 'intellectual model' (Sandow, 1994), showing what was important to them. The father was quietly observant, as he had been for most of the interview, according to my headteacher. The mother was looking more positive by the time I came in, and I reinforced what my headteacher and the EP (according to the parents) had said about not taking the scores too literally. Both parents grasped on to this and they began to be more positive about Jane's strengths: her learning progress (slow though it was), her excellent attitude to learning and her powers of concentration.

I thought the parents would be aggressive and blame the school for not teaching Jane to read as well as everyone else. They did not do this, though they quite possibly did at an earlier stage. At this time the father was positive and the mother patently agreeing; they were very keen that their daughter should remain at the school with all the support she needed to keep abreast of her peers, and they were willing to pay for it. They wanted to be sure that we would liaise and continue to provide the extra language skills support which Jane receives in school at present. I think they feared for their daughter's future which was also their own. They were aware that education can be bought, but not intelligence, but were prepared to do everything they could. They would have liked to apply the 'medical model' to provide reasons if not remedy. There had been a difficult birth but all developmental milestones had been normal. At least the 'social competence model' (Sandow, 1994) helped them to be more positive in that they would be content if she could keep up with her peers. These formal meetings make a very uneasy partnership from everyone's point of view, no doubt because we all feel threatened and fear to be blamed. However they begin to give me an insight into the primary system to which the child belongs, her immediate family, and more understanding of the complexity of her character and how to deal with her. Hopefully this will happen for the parents too so that trust and openness will develop. (R. S.)

Liaison with other professionals and with parents is very much part of the role of the teacher in the special school. There is no training for this, although the problems at the interface may be delicate as the following account of the induction of a new child with Down's syndrome into a class shows:

The issue I am interested in here is that of his hearing aids. He arrived with hearing aids and glasses in his school bag. The speech therapist showed me a report that indicated a significant hearing loss. His mother had told me that he didn't like wearing the hearing aids and that there are some situations which would be unpleasant for him to have them turned on in as well, e.g. lunch in the hall with a lot of noise. I decided that I wouldn't even suggest he wear them for at least a week whilst he settled into his new environment. Within two days both my assistant and myself were totally convinced that he can hear everything he wants to and he chooses to ignore the things he doesn't want to hear. You could see him actively ignore certain questions – there is no doubt he clearly understands what we say to him in sentences, although his hearing impairment can be seen when he is trying to make certain sounds – It is like the edges are blurred, and he can't distinguish between certain sounds. He will say that his baby brother is frying instead of crying. He picks up a lot from the context.

The teacher must negotiate between the parent and the speech therapist in the management of the hearing aids, for the latter has very different ideas, which are in conflict with the teacher's observations:

I spoke at length with his mother. She said that she feels that it is his human right not to wear them and tells him so she gives him free choice whether to wear them or not. I sympathise with this view, but it is not necessarily the best thing for the child. Next I arranged a meeting with the speech therapist who has known and worked with the child since he was eighteen months old. The first ten minutes of this meeting involved the speech therapist telling me that he **must** have the hearing aids in and switched on all day. I said I wasn't prepared to try and enforce this as I had to consider the whole child's development and not just from the speech therapist's view. He had by now reverted into a happy co-operative and confident child. I was now told that in the few months prior to coming to this school his behaviour had become unmanageable. He was kicking, spitting, biting, hitting, refusing to sit in class, refused to walk with a group. He was left to wander at will with no one saying 'no' to him. She also said that in terms of his hearing and speech development he should really wear them all the time or not at all so he would get a consistent hearing of sounds. All my instincts were to not use them at all, but I finally agreed that he should have his aids in all the time but only switched on in 'lesson' times, they could be switched off for play and lunch.

Managing the situation, the teacher finally trusted her own judgement and the hearing aids gradually fell into disuse. However, she ends with a wry question: 'Has he manipulated me or have I ensured that I am doing what I wanted to do in the first place?' (D. J.).

One professional who always arouses strong feelings is the educational psychologist. The duties imposed on the EP as a result of the 1993 Education Act have reduced even further the already limited time which the EP can spend actually advising teachers. The mystique which surrounds their work is often an irritant especially if time cannot be taken to explain results or indicate possible solutions to problems:

An EP visits our school three times per term only seeing pupils requiring statements. She meets with the class teacher for half an hour; sees the parents; observes the child; then returns to the office. There is no other contact. The school does not receive feedback from the visit either verbally or written. This contrasts with Mike's experience in which he said feedback was given to schools in 99% of cases, and verbal feedback was always given to the class teacher. Aubrey says that maybe EPs 'will be required to rekindle the psychometric tradition which never really died with Warnock in the 1980s' (Aubrey, 1994, p. 42). This certainly seems to be the case in our school. The Code of Practice says that 'in addition to examining the child, it may be necessary for the EP to observe the child over a period of time in order to formulate a clear picture of his or her needs' (DfE, 1994, para 3:114). This is not something that has happened in our institution. Teacher contact with the EP service in our school varies from minimal to none. It would be heartening to think that this situation was peculiar to us, however, a survey of the class on MSN1 (8/11/94) revealed that a proportionate number of teachers had never met their school's EP. This does not seem to accord with the view of the Association of EPs (AEP), which sees the role of the EP as one that transcends an 'assessment and disposal role' (Quicke, 1984, p. 125). Quicke's article seems very dated when he states that 'current emphasis is on a role that involves developing intervention strategies more directly useful to the class teacher in the ordinary school' (Quicke, p. 127). We seem to have passed through a forward thinking phase and now (due to restrictions of finance and demands imposed on EPs by the 1993 Act) are regressing to a less than satisfactory EP service. It seems appropriate at this point to remember the children; as Lucas says, their needs are at the 'focal point of our rationale for existence (Lucas, 1989, p. 173).

More and more we seem to be tied up with procedure and the children, our main concern, are no longer at the forefront of thinking. The Code of Practice says that 'the views of the EP are essential in fully assessing a child's Special Educational needs and in planning for any future problem' (DfE, 1994, para 3:113). This implies communication between EPs and teachers, as teachers need to be fully aware of a child's educational needs in order to meet them. Maybe EPs do not see it this way as communication can be non-existent. Gale asserts that 'Surely psychology is about enhancement of personal experience and self-esteem?' (Gale, 1991, p. 67). By not acknowledging the work teachers are doing and shutting them out of assessment procedures EPs are belittling and disempowering teachers, destroying rather than enhancing their self-esteem. Feiler talks of the mystique that often surrounds EPs. 'Why should so much power be conferred on groups of professionals who spend relatively little time in schools and whose role in the main thrust of the educational system is comparatively marginal?' (Feiler, 1988, p. 39). EPs would do well to take Gale's advice and acknowledge that 'To be successful with education we (EPs) need to persuade teachers, children, parents and governors that we can enter a partnership with them in achieving higher educational goals' (Gale, 1991, p. 71). I do acknowledge that EPs have tremendous case loads and are over worked . . . but aren't we all – is this an excuse? We are all working for the children – a multidisciplinary approach is essential, not an option. (O. J.)

When I have a child with either a learning or behavioural difficulty, I initially have high expectations of the educational psychologist; however, I am usually let down by what is actually done.

The educational psychologist will assess the child informally, then formally, then write a recommendation and send it to the school. These recommendations are usually vague and unhelpful reiterating what you as a class teacher already know and do. All of the staff feel that more explicit guidance is needed and more treatment carried out by the educational psychologist. Also there is a need for more lecturing and preventive work. Often the only time an educational psychologist has to talk to a teacher is in the classroom during a lesson – which is never a good time to talk. As a teacher you have very few opportunities for direct contact with an educational psychologist and so are unable to turn to her for advice on a child causing concern. More contact is needed over and above the infrequent school visits where just children are seen. Such findings by Lowenstein (1970) and Wright and Payne (1979) are echoed in many schools.

Our school gets only fifteen hours of educational psychologist time which means that we have a queue of children who need to be seen and it is a matter of prioritising who shall be seen this year or who will have to wait until next year.

However, schools therefore have expectations of the educational psychologist which are different from the psychologist's own idea of the role and when the school's expectations remain unfulfilled, often due to a lack of visits, conflict occurs between the school and the psychology service. (H. P.)

C. M. writes:

The school that I work in is a school for children with severe learning difficulties and the support we receive from the educational psychology service amounts to one half day per term. Practically all the children have statements of special educational need but these often need updating as the needs of the children change, after all, the children are with us from 5 to 19 years of age! We have to prioritise the children she sees as she normally sees only three if she is not meeting with parents and the children who are at the top of the list are invariably those with behaviour problems.

I have a five year old child in my class who has severe challenging behaviours which put herself and others at risk. She was prioritised for the next visit of the educational psychologist. Fortunately, due to some other child being away, the psychologist stayed with me for the whole morning and as a result was able to get a much clearer picture of the problems the child was displaying and also see how she was placing other children at risk. Even though the psychologist knew which child she was to see and I had sent her the many notes I had recorded about that child, together with the statement, she had not had the time to read them, so precious time was spent in the classroom while she did this. Prior to the visit I had written up some behavioural strategies for coping with the child and described how with added support for the child we could help her develop more acceptable behaviour patterns. I felt that the time I spent with the educational psychologist was invaluable as it reinforced the programmes I had already put into practice and she offered help and advice as and where they needed amending. Since her visit a year ago I have had no further contact with her and in fact due to reorganisation within that department she is no longer assigned to this school, but we are awaiting the appointment of a newly qualified educational psychologist. Though the reorganisation is intended to improve the service, I feel rather let down by the service as if I was to continue to meet this child's needs within the school her support and expertise would have been invaluable. Already in her short life this child has been under the care of four psychologists.

I believe that one of the ways forward would be for the educational psychology service to be based within schools for a far greater period than at present (Gale, 1991) and for that relationship to remain stable so that the educational psychologist to be able to build up relationships with the pupils and staff that they are trying to help. (C. M.)

However, sometimes, even with all the professionals working well together the child can seem to be a victim of the system. In this final example, confusion, impending change and mixed emotions militate against a successful outcome, even though all the correct procedures are followed. The events described happened before the advent of the Code of Practice. Mistrust, misunderstanding and conflicting advice eventually make it difficult for the teachers to resolve the problem:

H. is a year 2 child with complex needs which are difficult to assess. At the last review meeting, with the class teacher, Mrs R., the Ed Psych, and myself present at the meeting it was agreed that the Ed Psych would write a full report and in it state that had H. been staying in the borough we would have been requesting a formal assessment. After classroom observation, we initiated a meeting with mum to talk about H.'s difficulties and ways to help at home and at school. Mrs R. reported that H. had early hearing loss and was to have grommits fitted and have tonsil and adenoid treatment. I support in H.'s class for two hours a week and since that time most of this support has been targetted at H. Because of the early hearing loss we requested an assessment by the teacher for the hearing impaired who suggested that hearing was no longer a barrier to learning. Complicating the picture further H. began to demonstrate emotional behaviour problems. She was frustrated about her work and we discussed this with her mother and her new partner who reported that H. talked about death and about being fat and ugly. We agreed that she may be feeling insecure since the separation of her natural parents and would need lots of reassurance. Mum asked if H. might be dyslexic.

In June 1992 H. was assessed in school and some targets were set. At our multidisciplinary meeting it was agreed that we should refer H. for an informal assessment and a date was set for a meeting with Mrs R. on the same day. At this meeting a programme of work was recommended and a review date arranged. At this meeting mum again asked about dyslexia and the Ed Psych explained that we felt H.'s problems were more complex than that. We agreed to formal assessment and at this point Mrs R. told us that the family were moving to Cambridge and so it was decided to put the referral on hold but prepare a report for Mrs R. to take with her. The process of assessment is very lengthy and can be frustrating for all concerned. It is fair to say that we have kept Mrs R. informed of all procedures and involved her at each stage, though one could not describe the relationship as a partnership. Sandow (1987) suggests that parents seem to be seeking support from professionals but not necessarily an 'equal partnership' and this seems to apply in this case. The class teacher is concerned about H.'s emotional state but I suspect that the relationship between class teacher and H. mitigates against success. H. is not seen to behave in similar ways with other teachers. H. has had to come to terms with a period of unsettled family life, a 'new dad', moving house, etc. H. has a history of early hearing loss and she undoubtedly has learning difficulties. She has a poor self-image and is increasingly aware of the ability of her peers. All these features contribute to a unlikely climate for success. There have also been misunderstandings about behaviour management. The 'agreed' strategies failed to meet H.'s needs because they were misinterpreted and the tactics became negative and most unhelpful. I think that this indicates a need for some school based INSET and also a need for close monitoring and regular review. It is perhaps interesting to note that H. has been quite settled whilst working with a student teacher this term.

Recently Mrs R. took H. for an assessment at the Staines Dyslexia Institute and came away from there confused and distressed. Mr R. went with them and came in to school, for the first time since we had begun the assessment procedure, convinced that we had 'done nothing for two years', and demanding a formal assessment. At the end of the meeting with the parents we agreed to go ahead with a request for formal assessment on the grounds that the move to Cambridge had been delayed and because of the anxiety of the parents. Mrs R. was quite relieved to be able to call H.'s difficulties 'dyslexia', as if that was going to provide answer to her problems. As she said 'now we can do something about it'. (V. Q.)

CONCLUSION

These accounts and exchanges represent attempts at 'partnership' on the ground. The actuality appears to be more professionally directed than the shared expertise, responsibility and purpose suggested by Wolfendale (1989). However, they also demonstrate that the teacher identifies herself with the parent to a considerable extent and is aware of the anxieties expressed or unexpressed. In an account of parent perceptions of the statementing process (Sandow, 1987), it was suggested that parents were able to trust and relate to teachers and therapists more than to consulting professionals such as psychologists and psychiatrists. However, sometimes, as illustrated by the last extract, the search for an acceptable diagnosis leads to the rejection of a realistic way forward in favour of a fashionable solution. It is hard for teachers to resolve such problems (and keep cool) within a climate of accountability where parents are customers to be satisfied, as well as partners to be consulted and informed.

SECTION 3
Teachers and the Curriculum

Introduction

It is no secret that the curriculum has been and remains a battleground. In the mainstream the battle has been joined between the post-Plowden, child-centred Piagetians and the classical-humanist subject-based cultural transmission view of education. Currently, both views are in the process of being replaced by a competence-based view of education, in which a knowledge-based curriculum is delivered by teachers whose skills are identified in entirely pragmatic instrumental terms. It appears that teachers, while they reject this latest assault on their professionalism, find it hard to protest on the basis of a real understanding of their own preferred methods of teaching.

In special education, teachers are in a better position to fight the battles, and because teaching methods have been based in a clear understanding of the psychology and sociology of learning, they are better able to defend their professionalism. Effectively, there has emerged a compromise which could and should satisfy both the proponents of child-centred approaches and traditionalists. Whether it can survive the culture of naive pragmatism remains open to question.

Before the 1981 Education Act, special education took one of two forms: either it adopted a behavioural approach in teaching children social and cognitive skills on a 'need to know' basis, as in the former 'training centres' which were converted into schools after 1971, or in special classes in ordinary schools and in some special schools for children with emotional or behavioural difficulties it offered a largely therapeutic curriculum, attempting to support 'damaged' children through confidence building, while attempting to introduce a limited range of conventional subjects. In either case, teachers have been able to discuss their work in terms of intentions, processes and outcomes, rationally and imaginatively.

Both of these kinds of curricula were offered in a context of relatively full employment, and special schools could boast that they managed to place most of their pupils, at least immediately after leaving school, in some sort of job. Often employers actively sought to engage school-leavers from these establishments.

Now things are different. With high levels of unemployment among the under twenty-fives, graduates of special schools are often at the back of the queue for jobs. The advent of the National Curriculum and the concept of entitlement have

65

forced teachers in special education, as well as those in the mainstream, to reappraise their priorities, and reconsider their methods. In many ways they are more able to do this constructively than are other teachers.

This section includes four chapters in which teachers look critically at the way they teach and about the appropriateness of the curriculum itself. Should children be offered the whole of the National Curriculum as of right even if it has to be manipulated to fit the way the special schools operate? Has behavioural pedagogy anything to offer the mainstream teacher attempting to reconcile the excitement of discovery with the skills of a competence-based curriculum? It is often said that methods which are good for children who have special needs are actually methods which are good for all children. The organisation and observation necessary in the construction of an Individual Education Plan only demonstrates, clearly, the processes which take place in the planning of an 'ordinary' whole-class curriculum.

Davies (1994) has drawn attention to the 'mainsprings of fatalism and deference' which have contributed to the pusillanimity with which society and the schools and teachers within it have accepted the criticism of methods and outcomes from the publication of the Black Papers in the 1960s. There have, he writes, been 'thirty years of under-theorised curriculum innovation' which have left teachers ill-prepared to respond with confidence to such strictures. 'If all you have before you is your own (and historically filtered) practice, it is unlikely to become an object for more than superficial technical inspection.'

This has certainly not been true of teachers in special education. Their practice has been well theorised and constantly examined and refined, as the entries in the following pages will show. So special education has a great deal to offer in observing and identifying the teaching and learning process, and in the definition of techniques of teaching which do not deny professional artistry but complement it.

5

Teachers and Differentiation

The National Curriculum provoked much anxiety among teachers of children with special needs, both in ordinary and in special schools. Although at first it was widely assumed that there would be much disapplication of the NC, especially in special schools, that has not been the case. Certainly among some SLD teachers, it has been argued that the NC is largely an irrelevance (Hinchcliffe, 1994) being incompatible with the mainly developmental curriculum being followed in such schools. A group of teachers following an in-service course in the SLD curriculum identified a number of serious anxieties when reviewing Curriculum Guidance 9 The National Curriculum and Pupils with Severe Learning Difficulties (Hinchcliffe et al., 1992):

It is precisely this principle of entitlement and the relevance of POS to children with profound learning difficulties that are critically discussed here. This group has questioned both the way that the principle of 'entitlement' has been taken on board by SLD schools and how this principle has almost been treated with reverence in the wealth of literature published in the wake of the 1988 ERA. Members of this group, all teaching children with profound and multiple difficulties, have been grappling with the initiatives of the ERA in the classroom and are becoming increasingly sceptical as to whose interests the National Curriculum ATs and POS are serving. It is maintained that whatever the arguments of a centrally imposed curriculum for raising standards in mainstream schools, the relevance of all of this to children with profound and multiple learning difficulties is highly debatable. It seems that only a few people, in print anyway, are prepared to challenge and debate its relevance.

The NCC states that when the NC was being formulated, 'it was impossible to legislate for the enormous diversity of special educational needs'. We believe this statement to be both a simplification and a retrospective 'cop out'. Few, if any, members of the National Curriculum Working Party can have had experience of teaching children with severe learning difficulties . . .

Why should teachers of children with PMLD have to mould existing good practice to POS which, in the main were not written for, and are arguably, not relevant to this client group? Some tenuous links of common practice to National Curriculum POS are seen in this NCC document. In the section on suggested methods of doing a curriculum audit, a 'clap hands' singing activity is described in which a child in a group is seen to fall off his chair. The NCC's National Curriculum POS references to these events are 'responding to aural stimuli', 'exploring how to make and experience sounds', and 'receiving explanations' (presumably, why the student fell off his chair). Is this type of referencing really necessary? It rather suggests milking NC Programmes of Study for a relevance that is not really there, and this ignorance is reflected in the token references to the needs and interests of these children.

So as far as children with SLD are concerned, it appears that these teachers believe that differentiation of a common curriculum leaves too many needs unaddressed in the scramble for entitlement. S. J. (1992) also argued against the relevance of the NC, and cited parents' as well as teachers' anxieties. Teachers made the following points:

It's too rigid, it doesn't take into account the students individual needs. The curriculum may become too structured. When teaching children with SLD, a teacher should be able to continue and develop a lesson provided that there is positive interest and stimulation for the pupils. It is inhibiting to have to change a lesson in order to cover the whole of the NC. The NC subject divisions do not take into account the way children with SLD need to be taught (real situations with cross curricular input) or what they really need to be learning (life skills). It does not start at an early enough stage of development. Some children will be working towards level one for the whole of their school career, for them it does not provide a framework for progression in learning, they just fail.

However, others take the view that children with SLD can and should be given access to the NC as a matter of right. They should, according to T. P.:

be treated as active learners. To be able to get the most out of education they must be able to interact with people and their environment. Fagg et al. (1990) stress the importance of interaction and communication in giving pupils with SLD access to the NC. 'The NC documents currently available all assume within their content, a level of growth of interpersonal and communicative skills which are central to the achievement of the programmes of study and attainment targets.' For pupils with SLD this cannot be assumed. Pupils must be helped to develop the skills. Teachers should create the opportunities, through chosen activities, for pupils to learn and practise interactive skills.

D. D. also stresses the importance of interactive skills in work with autistic children, noting that hierarchical learning (such as in the NC) causes problems where development is not simply delayed but is also distorted or uneven. Considering the needs of Katie, an autistic child, she writes:

It is important not to disapply children like Katie from the National Curriculum. One concern if this comes about is that they may be deemed ineducable. The other concern is that the child's entitlement to the National Curriculum is denied. Jordan and Powell (1990) described autistic children as having a 'distorted rather than merely delayed pattern of development. This (they said) causes difficulties whenever learning is organised into hierarchies as in the National Curriculum'. Obviously the National Curriculum has completely changed the structure of the learning environment in schools such as this one. However, for the children who do not fit the hierarchy there needs to be opportunity to provide them with strategies to develop.

There is a need for functional contexts to ensure learned skills are generalised. This is especially relevant in role play and other language orientated situations, e.g. setting a context for language. In a teasing/jokes situation, Katie needs to know what response is required at home or at school, so that she avoids moments of confusion that generally lead to confrontation.

Specific training is quite often required. This is illustrated in the role play, ability to reason and dealing with teasing and jokes. In these instances Katie is given a set way of responding and as this is established opportunities to generalise these skills are developed.

It is also essential to create a thinking environment for a child like Katie. The sequencing objective is to assist in establishing this. Katie's major difficulty is in organising her thoughts and she is inclined to lean heavily on adults or other children for prompts in difficulties. This is the most important element of Katie's learning programme. Because she is so fragmented it would be easy to concentrate on the negative elements and use these as an excuse for little progress. It is far more honest and positive to recognise that Katie's learning might be slow and inconsistent at the moment but as she matures and becomes more organised her learning may become quicker.

Clearly, such attention to detail and recognition of differently paced learning is hard to reconcile with the need to cover a wide range of subjects and activities as required by the NC.

However, some teachers are more sanguine about the possibilities of working within the NC. Even children with PMLD are considered by O. J. (1993) to be able to learn within this framework. O. J. describes work at KS1 in Science carried out with a group of non-ambulant preverbal children with PMLD. She regards 'entitlement' as a positive thing, but recognises that 'it is not always appropriate for all of these children to be restricted to the topics and content directed by the Science NC'. O. J. continues to describe her work by looking at the principles of the NC in the light of learning theorists. Here O. J. shows the advantages of theorising out of practice, rather than in advance of it: it is obvious that she has observed and explored the child's learning and then related it to theory:

It is interesting that the majority of those special schools that have been stated by OFSTED to have failed inspection, have done so primarily for not adhering to the National Curriculum.

Are the sentiments behind Curriculum Guidance 9 based on empty statements? The worst scenario is that the NCC have no understanding of the needs of children with PMLD, and are going to recommend schools to teach inappropriate material, to the detriment of our pupils' education. I can justify my KS1 unit in terms of the National Curriculum but more importantly, it has been devised after assessing the needs of the pupils. I would not advocate teaching all of Level 1 science to this class, nor will I be restricted by specific learning outcomes. The unit is child-centred, based on relevant aims and objectives.

The children in this class are functioning at very early levels of development, five of them corresponding developmentally to Piaget's sensory-motor period (relating to the first two years of life in a normally developing child). Mike is fairly typical, developmentally, of the children in this class. He is functioning in stages two, three and the lower portion of 4 according to the Uzgiris and Hunt scales of infant psychological development. Mike can be very vocal but scored low on vocal imitation, as he did on gestural imitation – his development is particularly behind in this area. He does not interact with people. Mike does not seem to make the distinction between people and objects. Mike's assessment has been included to give a clearer indication of the developmental level of the children in this class. The sixth child in the class is more advanced than the sensory-motor stage but as she started school for the first time this year (she is almost 11 years old) she has a lot to learn. We are not clear at this stage how much the absence of education and limited exposure to some language is affecting her responses.

If we accept Bruner's assertion that 'any subject can be taught effectively in some intellectually honest form to any child at any stage in development' (Bruner, 1963), the problem is not whether or not to teach science (a hypothetical question as the National Curriculum does not allow us this choice – unless the child has been disapplied) but how to teach it. The first principle drawn from Piaget's theory is the view that learning has to be an active process because knowledge is a construction from within (Schwebel et al., 1974, p. 99). Both Bruner and Vygotsky agreed that action is important in cognitive development but unlike Piaget, they did not adhere to the view that educators should wait for the children to be ready to learn (Smith, 1988). A teaching programme for this class must be active and involve the children in intervention from, and interaction with other people. The children's chronological ages bear little relation to their psychological development – as educators we must intervene and try to facilitate development. I think it is important to consider Vygotsky's theory of the Zone of Proximal Development (ZPD). The ZPD 'focuses on the phase in development in which the child has only partially mastered a task but can participate in its execution with the assistance and supervision of an adult or more capable peer' (Rogoff et al., 1984, p. 1). It is the 'distance between the level of performance that a child can reach unaided and the level of participation that she or he can accomplish when guided by another more knowledgeable individual' (Rogoff et al., 1984, p. 77). The ZPD is concerned with a child's potential developmental levels. Bruner expressed a similar idea with his metaphor 'scaffolding', in which not only a child's existing level is taken into account, but how far they can progress with help (Smith, 1988). ZPD and scaffolding bring to the fore the notion of 'potential' development and the importance of intervention to achieve this. A teaching programme must attempt to move the children forward. It is also relevant to keep in mind Bruner's Spiral Curriculum i.e. that knowledge arises out of a process of deepening understanding. He implied that even quite young children could grasp ideas in an intuitive way which they could return to later and move progressively towards more complex levels of difficulty (Smith, 1988). Therefore what we teach the children can be built on later. There may not be any immediate, visible learning outcomes, but, according to the Spiral Curriculum, the pupils can build on their experiences in the future.

The pupils in this particular class will be working within Key Stage One of the Science Curriculum. There are four Attainment Targets – I have chosen to teach a unit from Life and Living Processes, Attainment Target two. This unit will focus on the children's own bodies and their senses. This area of learning is important for the children in addition to meeting the requirements of the National Curriculum. 'Sensory input initiates perception' (Brown, 1977, p. 48). The unit will be on 'Our bodies' but will focus on what our bodies can do, i.e. the senses.

The Science Curriculum states that 'To communicate, to relate science to everyday life and to explore are essential elements of an initial experience of science, (Science in the National Curriculum 1991). This unit will use materials from the immediate environment (as far as possible) and explore those materials using all the senses. To avoid sensory confusion the lessons will attempt to focus on one sense at a time. The School Physiotherapist, Nurse, and Speech Therapist will be asked to assist and give advice in three of the sessions. It is important to consult other professionals when planning any programme.

Children's skills and concepts in science are developed best through an active rather than passive approach and especially through exploration and interaction with their environment (Benson, 1991 in Smith, 1988, p. 48). This teaching unit is based entirely around activities (also in accordance with Piaget, Vygotsky and Bruner's views about active learning). Although this unit was primarily written for the science curriculum it has cross-curricular links. This is important as subjects should not be seen as separate entities taught in isolation – education should be round/whole. For a subject to be relevant it must have links with other curriculum areas. This unit will incorporate aspects of Physical Education, Drama, PSHE, IT, Art, Communication and Language. 'An important feature of an interactive approach is the acquisition and development of language skills. By using relevant and varied contexts within which to set activities, the understanding and acquisition of language concepts should be enhanced' (Benson, 1991 in Smith, 1988, p. 48). Language used with the children must of course be relevant. All of the children are preverbal so while it will be important to explain what is going on and ensure the pupils are familiar with the parts of their bodies and object labels (names of objects) these instructions must be kept simple and to the point. It will be as important for staff to be sensitive to and respond to the children's own vocalisations or other forms of response, to encourage the development of intentional communication.

Following this introduction, O. J. describes a comprehensive programme which moves from whole body awareness to specific exploration of hands and feet, always differentiating the experiences to take account of children's likes and dislikes. Finally the focus moves to exploring the other senses: vision, hearing, taste and smell. The detailed programme is included here to illustrate the high level of detail with which teachers of children with PMLD plan and carry out their curricula:

Our Bodies:
A Science Unit, working in Key Stage 1, Attainment Target 2, specifically designed for students with PMLD.
The Unit is divided into 11 lessons, however some may need repeating to reinforce ideas or to capitalise on positive experiences.

Aims:
For the pupils:
– to find out about themselves
– to be aware of their whole body
– to recognise names of body parts
– to develop ideas of what their bodies can do
– to enjoy stimulation of the senses.

Objectives:
For the pupils:
• to focus on own body.
• to become familiar with the names of body parts.
• to respond to stimulation of the senses.
• to have positive experiences.

Before the Unit:
– Collect/take photos of each child in the class.
– Tape the voices of the children in the class.
– Sew tinsel, bells, bright pompoms, fur; glue on glitter to gloves and socks.
– Consult with Physiotherapists, Nurse and Speech Therapist.
– Make feely bags.
– Discuss Aims and Objectives of the Unit with Support Staff.

Activities:
1. Focus – Whole body.
Use 'TacPac' – this lesson will take about an hour to complete. Begin by singing 'Hallo'.
   Follow the instructions in the pack. Make sure that the room is warm and that all the equipment is ready before the lesson.
2. Focus – Body/try to recognise self and others.
Use 'Good Morning' session – look at photos of self and others. Pupils try to

select own photo from choice of two (R.'s photo has fur on it; T.'s has bells as they are visually impaired).

This activity will be used every morning.

Outline of bodies – Children lie on a large piece of paper (individually) and outline is made of their bodies. Go around bodies several times with a big paintbrush or broom (not with paint!) so that they feel their outline. Show pupils the outlines (these could be painted in an Art session).

Have Physiotherapist go through simple stretching exercises – sing songs e.g. 'I've got a body'.

3. Focus – Movement; kinaesthetic and vestibular.
Concentrate on the words: swing, backwards, forwards, round, up, down, slide.

Begin with the 'Roller Coaster' game (instructions in the 'Fun Fair' pack) – to bring children together as a group and introduce movement. Put soft play equipment around hall to make the game more exciting.

Swing the children (individually!) in a blanket – sing: 'What shall we do with . . .'.

Slide along floor in a sack or on a blanket.

Slide down playground slides – using both the metal and roller ones.

Spin on a rotating chair.

It would be preferable to begin with all the children watching each other but if they are not focused or lose interest, the group can split and go ahead with activities (all children will need two staff for lifting etc).

4. Focus – Hands.
Begin by massaging hands.

Put prepared gloves on children's hands – take time to try and put all fingers in. If necessary use velcro to keep gloves on – do not do this if the child shows any signs of distress.

Take gloves off and look at hands through magnifying glasses.

Turn lights off and focus on hands with torch beams.

Put paint on hands – encourage children to do this themselves – make hand prints.

5. Focus – Hands.
Begin by massaging hands. Use gloves as in previous lesson.

Have children put their hands into feely bags – encourage them to explore themselves.

Verbal then physical prompts – do not force.

Put paint on hands – encourage children to do this themselves – make hand prints.

6. Focus – Feet.
Begin by massaging feet. Use socks as in previous lesson.

Put prepared socks on children's feet. Encourage them to look.

Take socks off. Put paint on feet – encourage children to do as much as they can on their own. Make feet prints.

Encourage the children to put their feet into the feely bags – use verbal then physical prompts, but do not force.

7. Focus – Feet

Begin by massaging feet. Use socks as in previous lesson.

Encourage the children to put their feet into the feely bags – use verbal then physical prompts, do not force.

8. Focus – Eyes.

Begin by putting hats on and looking in the mirror – sing 'R.'s got a black hat . . .'.

Put glasses on the children, use bright rimmed glasses/sunglasses/glasses made in Art session – look in the mirror – sing 'My eyes are dim, I cannot see . . .'.

In a dark room use torches and ultra-violet light to focus on themselves/objects.

9. Focus – Hearing.

Begin as in previous lesson with hats and song etc.

Use the mirror to look at ears – use false ears/ear-muffs.

Listening activities – 'Walkmans' (tapes of own voices + music, songs), musical bumps, stethoscope, large shells etc. Use the Resonance Board for the visually impaired.

10. Focus – Taste and Smell.

Begin again with hats etc.

Put coloured sunblock on noses – put on children's fingers and encourage them to put it on themselves – use the mirror.

Speech Therapist to lead tasting session.

11. Focus – Taste and Smell.

Begin with hats etc. Put on sunblock as in previous lesson.

School Nurse to lead teeth cleaning session.

Throughout, O. J. stresses the importance of evaluating both the teaching and the learning that is going on. The whole unit is designed so that the children will be aware of their bodies and are able to discriminate between their senses: it fits easily into the National Curriculum.

These detailed programmes demonstrate that the curriculum, including the National Curriculum, can be used to give a framework for teaching 'in an intellectually honest way' at any level. This is not simply a matter of differentiation in the conventional sense, but of identifying the starting points and learning programmes for a number of children working together, and producing programmes which are individual but also highly social, true child-centred learning, in fact. Where teachers are faced with learning difficulties in the mainstream, these programmes may seem the height of luxury. It is, however, possible to draw lessons from the examples about how IEPs are constructed, from the inside out – at any level. For example, another teacher (A. B.) views differentiation as part of her task as a support teacher in secondary history classes. She sees differentiation as part of the process of improving teaching and learning for all pupils, but rejects the use of the term to segregate children within an overtly inclusive system. To me an emphasis on meeting individual needs does not have to be packaged up with efforts to 'sort and separate' children. Differentiation is perceived as 'giving an opportunity for children with different strengths and weaknesses to participate in the same learning activity, in different ways'.

A. B. applied this principle to a session on the abolition of slavery, one of a series in which children at KS3 had already considered the slave resistance movement. Working with a 'bottom set' it is notable that she recognised that individual differences required different options for children with different abilities and communication skills:

This lesson aimed to develop pupils' awareness that there can be a number of different reasons or causes for events and that these can be interconnected.

More specifically, it was intended to help pupils to develop or further their understanding of certain concepts/terminology with which they may not yet be very familiar, such as 'economic', 'politican', 'humanitarian' and 'religious' motives for actions. It also aimed to develop some knowledge about the ideas and beliefs which drove the sequence of events which led to the abolition of the slave trade and emancipation of the slaves in British colonies and, later, in the USA.

The children are all in a bottom set, but they still obviously differ with regard to many factors such as literacy, ability to communicate ideas orally, general grasp of concepts, relevant background knowledge and vocabulary, interest and commitment to the subject, ability to work cooperatively with other children, etc. In this lesson, I wanted to enable those who have very low levels of literacy to learn and demonstrate their knowledge and understanding, and to minimise the burden of reading and writing. I wanted to provide the opportunity for those who have particular strengths in oral work to make a contribution that might not be made so well through their written work. I chose to incorporate a few quick and easy informal brief 'tests' with minimal literacy demands to obtain some evidence to indicate which children may still not understand some of the key concepts. This information can be used to guide their next lesson. I also made assessments of other factors such as level of engagement and degree of success with various tasks, so that I could hopefully tailor future lessons more closely to individual needs.

Main differentiation methods

I wished to enable children with very low levels of literacy to participate in the same intellectual task as all the other pupils, so I tried to create a few different kinds of opportunities to obtain information and to demonstrate understanding within a whole class activity.

'Considerate' text – conversation scripts

For listening or reading I used a conversation format to cover main points mentioned through four or five chapters of the textbook used in the school (Heinemann History: Black Peoples of the Americas, 1992). The main strategies I tried to use in making the scripts included: avoiding unrealistic assumptions about background knowledge; making connections between motives and actions more explicit; deletion of excess detail; inclusion of familiar images to aid mental representation of more abstract ideas; use of familiar language and references as much as possible; replacing unfamiliar vocabulary items and words that moderately poor readers might find difficult to decode or listeners to understand.

The scripts could be 'accessed' either by reading or listening, depending on the abilities of the individual childen. The task connected with the scripts was a categorisation one which minimised literacy demands while focusing attention on important terms that will be later encountered frequently in history. These terms were also taught explicitly beforehand.

Speech preparation and delivery, using pupils' strengths for collaborative small group work
The task of preparing a speech in a small group could enable each group member to contribute an idea or suggestion and interact with the ideas of others even though only one scribe was needed. It could also allow group members who did not really grasp the concepts or information at the presentation stage of the lesson to clarify their understanding through small group interaction with peers.

The actual delivery of the speech provided an opportunity for any group member who had the confidence to give a speech in front of the class to do so, even if they couldn't read the speech and had to rely on memory. I knew that several of the statemented pupils do have this oral confidence. They should be able to draw on all the new concepts and information encountered in the lesson.

Repetition of key points in different ways. The summary gap fill sheet gave a more straightforward, text book-like account of events and the reasons for them. This was planned to come after the explicit teaching of terminology and after the illustrative conversation scripts. I wanted to explicitly teach meanings of words 'economic', 'political', 'humanitarian' and 'religious', so that the children could supply the definition and, later, correctly apply these words to a situation. (I expected that all the children would know what 'religious' means but that many would have, at best, only a vague awareness of the other terms, particularly 'economic'.) I wanted to repeat these four terms quite frequently so that the children would understand them and feel less threatened when they encountered them in their reading. One way to do this was to get them to categorise each speech as illustrating one or more of these motives for wanting to end slavery. This involved listening and thinking but hardly any writing (they only had to choose the correct word and copy it into a chart).

Pupil grouping. I had intended to choose group members in order to achieve a balance of abilities for the task of preparing the speech. (Although the pupils ended up choosing their own groups, they chose quite well and a balance of abilities, especially to do with literacy, was present in all groupings.)

Varied assessment and recording methods planned
- Chart filled in by pupils with the instruction 'treat this like a test and do your own'.
- Pupil speeches (photocopies provided later by teacher to put in exercise books).
- Gap-fill for revision summary without need for time consuming copying.
- True/false (minimal written response).
- Teacher ratings of involvement, behaviour and quality of pupil talk.

Activity one Whole class – questions by teacher, eliciting background knowledge the children already have.

Introduce theme: 'Why did some white people want to end slavery?' Explicitly teach simple definitions of 'economic', 'political', 'humanitarian' and 'religious' reasons.

Activity two Pupils listen to definitions and/or read them on sheet. Alert pupils to need to listen to conversation scripts to work out what reasons were being put forward in each one. State that in some cases there might be more than one reason.

Tell pupils they will later be preparing their own speeches in groups so they should listen carefully to the conversations because they will be making similar points in their speeches.

Activity three Conversation scripts – get the better readers (volunteers) to read them. Some pupils read scripts aloud, others listen.

Activity four All pupils choose and write/copy correct word(s). Tell pupils to fill in the chart using one or more of the given words, after they hear each conversation, as a kind of test.

Activity five Small group task – some to make oral contribution of ideas, one to be scribe for group production of anti-slavery speech.

Give instructions for a group task on making a speech against slavery, using all four categories of reasons, using any information they have been given this lesson or in previous lessons. One person to write, all to contribute.

Make groups of three, ensuring that each contains one child with adequate ability to be a scribe. Aim for a mix of ability to grasp concepts. Both teachers go round to monitor group work, remind them about goal of including all four categories of reason in their speech, check understanding, ensuring that all members have a role.

Activity Six Whole class listen to all the speeches. Pupils can decide which group member will deliver the speech, but the teachers should encourage someone who has difficulty reading to do it from memory (in other words, not the scribe).

All speech makers to be listened to carefully and applauded. Pupils to be given a photocopy of all group speeches later (supplied by teacher).

Activity seven Whole class reading or listening to summary of events read out by teacher, then completing gap-fill together.

Give out gap-fill summary sheet (Activity three) 'British opposition to slavery in the Americas'. Do as whole class exercise, reading text aloud, filling gaps as we go, on the sheet. This can be used as a timeline exercise if time is available at end of lesson.

Note: The purpose of this gap-fill was mainly to avoid time spent copying the summary which is needed in the exercise book for possible exam revision later. Providing it this way was intended to focus their attention more than if there were no gaps and to allow for further checking of comprehension and consolidation of main points by teacher.

Activity eight Whole class reading or listening to check understanding through minimal writing response.

Give out 'True or false' sheet (Similar purpose to gap-fill). Pupils listen or read the sentence pairs and write down the letter (a) or (b).

If time, they can then *either* copy out the true ones into their exercise books *or* paraphrase the correct sentences in their own words *or* slower writers could cross out the false ones and stick the sheet in their book so that only the correct ones remain for later revision.

CONCLUSION

The range of activities described in this chapter illustrates the way in which teachers have taken on board differentiation by input, process and outcome, in ways which make a great number of curricular topics accessible for pupils of all levels of ability. The modifications contained in the 'Dearing version' of the NC will hopefully free teachers to develop the sorts of innovations described here. Some teachers of pupils with severe learning difficulties may still fret at what they see as an unnatural alignment of some aspects of the SLD curriculum to fit the NC, but some developments, such as the science topic elaborated here, show how the framework can give structure to existing content and stimulate powers of invention. In the ordinary school, the detailed description of a differentiated history curriculum is surely infinitely preferable to yet more 'basics' delivered by despairing teachers to bored pupils denied the more interesting activities in which their classmates participate.

6

Teachers Using Behavioural and Interactive Methods: Lessons from the SLD School

Professional knowledge in the field of teaching children with severe learning difficulties is still in its infancy. State schools for children with severe learning difficulties have only been in existence for 24 years. The passing of the 1970 Education (Handicapped Children) Act officially admitted children with severe learning difficulties into the education system. The influence of pedagogy with children with SLD in the mainstream school has been minimal; most ordinary schools have little idea of the techniques used, or how they might have value in the mainstream. Newly qualified teachers usually know little of what happens behind the doors of special schools (Garner, 1994). Now that the Individual Education Plan (IEP) has been enshrined in the Code of Practice, the experiences of teachers in SLD schools deserve to be more widely known.

In the 1970s one of the authors (V. H.) was among one of the first cohorts of student teachers in higher education following the new B.Ed. ESN(S) course. These courses and the Cert. Eds. before them were developed to meet the training needs of this new school population of children in ESN (S) schools. It was a specialist course. All of those on the course intended to teach children with severe learning difficulties; this was why they were on the course. Many had been working with such children for years. At the same time another of us (S. S.) was similarly consolidating practical experiences in SLD schools with academic study.

For V. H. in addition to the main subject study (mental handicap, as it was called in those days), there was also a generic mainstream component, for example the junior curriculum. What was special about the main subject study was its departure from the mainstream curriculum. On this specialist component (representing a third of the course), students did not learn more about the mainstream curriculum, they learned about teaching and learning specific to children with severe learning difficulties. At that time, they were introduced to behavioural methodology, as behavioural-product teaching approaches were dominant in special schools. However, despite this rather narrow focus, at that time, curriculum practice for this group of children was seen as essentially different from that of mainstream schools. At the other end of the country, S. S. was learning at university that the methods she had been developing to assist the severely 'handicapped' and autistic children she taught had a 'scientific' basis in classical psychology.

Looking back through old lecture notes, one can clearly see how we were influenced by the 'medical model'. We were young and keen. We were the new breed of special educators. We were trained in behavioural techniques, and with checklists in hand we went out into schools to show how we could remediate children's learning difficulties. Of course, on teaching practice, it did not take long to realise that teaching and learning involves a lot more than this. However, the essential principles of a behavioural methodology served us well. We learned to be systematic in observation and assessment. We had learned to prioritise teaching and learning in an attempt to meet children's very individual needs. In those days, it would have been a shocking concept to consider offering children in special schools a 'watered-down' mainstream curriculum. It seems ironic that fifteen years on, post-National Curriculum, to a large extent that is exactly what teachers working in special schools are expected to do. Chapter 5 illustrates some present day anxieties over this. Are we really saying that, in the relatively short history of special education (less than twenty-five years), children with severe learning difficulties benefit from a mainstream curriculum?

BEHAVIOURAL-PRODUCT APPROACHES

When children with severe learning difficulties were officially admitted into the education system, behavioural-product approaches, mainly originating from the work of B. F. Skinner in the United States, dominated teaching and learning in special education. The work of special educators like Bender and Valletutti (1982) gave teachers a framework to separate curricular areas, isolate skills and break them down into behavioural objectives. Here, the teacher was concerned with observable behaviour, behaviour which could be measured. A 'task analysis' was used to describe the task in behavioural terms, then isolate, sequence and slice the task or skill into its component parts. Specific objectives were devised so that mastery could be determined within given criteria for success. After having analysed the task, teachers could use a range of behavioural techniques to teach behaviour, e.g., chaining, shaping, prompting and errorless discrimination learning.

U. B. provides a useful summary of these techniques:

- Chaining: Some tasks lend themselves to this technique. These tend to be tasks which contain many components, each of which can be performed on their own. Backward chaining can be used to enable the student to experience the success of finishing the task independently, particularly useful when teaching dressing and undressing.
- Shaping: This strategy is also used for teaching complex tasks. After the task has been broken down into its component skills, these skills are reconsidered. If this reveals to the teacher that the tasks are still too complex,

it may be necessary to use specially prepared materials which offer opportunities for the child to practise the skill, using larger than life simulations, e.g., larger buttons on a coat.

- Errorless discrimination learning: This can be used to bring an element of fun to behavioural programmes. Initially, it involves providing a context in which the child cannot fail, however, it can lead on to the introduction of 'red herrings'. Careful observation of the response of the student when these are used can provide valuable information on the way he or she is reading the situation.

- Prompts and cues: Different levels of prompts can be used to keep the student on task and guide them towards success – verbal, gestural or physical.

In the 1970s and early 1980s the behavioural approach using such techniques found favour in British special schools. It gave teachers structure and, in many ways, offered them the security of detailed checklists on which ticks and prompt codes could be completed. It provided teachers with a long-term perspective and carried with it the expectations of success. Task analysis often reveals how complex it is to 'unpack' some of the skills that we may take for granted (Ouvry, 1991).

Behavioural methods were seen to be effective. Intensive teaching in dedicated environments (e.g., in stimulus free rooms) demonstrated that children's behaviour could be relatively easily modified (Skinner had demonstrated this in the 1950s). Those of us who taught in schools at this time tended to ignore the fact that when such external reinforcement was removed, and when children were observed in natural environments (e.g., in the home), generalisation of these learned behaviours often proved to be weak. The solution was seen to be the importation of the same techniques into the home, via home teachers who initiated parents into behavioural techniques. The Portage Project (Shearer, 1972), still extant and popularised through Education Support Grants, is a reminder of those days, though today it has softened the greater rigidities of its approach.

The popularity of behavioural methodology could be seen across the curriculum; from self-help programmes to teaching numeracy. Most of the commercial teaching schemes published in the early 1980s stressed the importance of using the behavioural approach. These included The Education of the Developmentally Young (Foxen and McBrien, 1981) and Portage itself (Bluma et al., 1976). Even some higher order mental processes, including language, were subjected to a behavioural methodology (see Leeming et al., 1979).

INTERACTIVE-PROCESS APPROACHES

Towards the end of the 1980s, greater interest was shown in what Smith (1987, 1990) called interactive-process approaches to teaching. The process model was not new, of course. Stenhouse (1975) and Eisner's (1985) work on what they called 'expressive objectives' was known but special education was too young and the behavioural influence too strong for process methods to be taken seriously. However, by the 1990s there was a plethora of publications which challenged the behavioural tradition (Smith, 1987, 1991; Coupe and Goldbart, 1988; Hewett and Nind (1992); Tilstone (1991). Concern was expressed about the high levels of adult direction and external control often associated with behaviourism. Questions were raised about how children could be more involved in their own learning, how they could demonstrate more self-control and self-determination. There were also concerns about both the transfer and relevance of some behavioural programmes. There was a danger that some of these may have focused on narrow and possibly inconsequential aspects of learning, and the relevance of some of these to the lives of some severely disabled children was questionable.

K. N., writing from personal experience, describes how she has seen children become over-dependent on prompts:

Prompting must be seen to be providing real help to the pupil in learning the task; if this is not clearly the case then the use of prompts needs to be re-evaluated. Prompting can prove to be counter-productive and lead the child to a level of learned dependency, i.e., when the child becomes dependent on the prompt to perform the task. (see Ager, 1989)

The process-content movement in education and the concerns about how a rigidly applied behavioural approach can lead to an imbalance of power between adult and child reflected the advocacy movement of the 1990s. The Children Act (1989) shifted the balance of power to the child, as Corbett (1994) states, giving 'status, credibility and strength to children, who traditionally have been a powerless and oppressed social group'. Clements (1987) talked about the need for modified expectations towards people with severe learning disabilities, viewing them as 'people with a potential for self-efficacy, rather than as being forever passive and dependent, requiring a high degree of external control'. Winchurst et al. (1992) describe the environmental factors which historically have militated against such self-determination – 'a person's lack of exposure to "real-life" social interaction, differential (often patronising) treatment from others, and therefore infrequent opportunities to make and express real choices'.

Behavioural approaches were most readily criticised in the teaching of language and communication. In fact it is difficult to conceive of language being 'taught'; although much can be done to provide opportunities and contexts in which language can develop. The work of Harris (1987, 1993, 1994), Hewett and Nind (1987, 1992), Coupe and Goldbart (1988) in the late 1980s and early 1990s did much to promote the role of pragmatics in developing language and communication in special education. Pragmatics concerns the social functions of language – what children can do with their existing communication, how and when they make demands on their environment and the people within it. This focus represents a shift from teaching language performance within stimulus-response procedures, for example, in 'dead-end' object labelling exchanges. Teachers were less preoccupied with achieving a match between teacher language and child language within grammarian language programmes. The emphasis switched to providing a richer learning environment, creating opportunities for problem-solving, choice-making and peer interaction (Goldbart, 1988).

Children's 'thinking skills', that is, their ability to monitor and organise their own learning in problem-solving situations, seems to be a neglected area in interactive approaches to teaching and learning. Borkowski's (1983, 1984) research into metacognition was taken up by the Staff of Rectory Paddock School (1983) in an attempt to teach children to use a number of strategies to evaluate the effectiveness of their own learning. After a period of instruction, children were encouraged to use a number of self-initiated strategies to monitor their own problem-solving strategies.

U. B. talks about metacognitive processes and how children should be encouraged to take more control of their own learning, to reflect upon their knowledge and understanding:

the basic skills of metacognition include predicting the consequences of an action or event, checking the results of one's own actions (did it work?), monitoring one's ongoing activity (how am I doing?), reality testing (does this make sense?) and a variety of other behaviours for co-ordinating and controlling deliberate attempts to learn and solve problems.

She goes on to state that such self-monitoring skills 'enable students to transfer knowledge from former experiences . . . They must learn skills, but they must also learn how, when and why these skills can be utilised in the real world.'

A real-life example of some work aimed at encouraging a child to devise such strategies for problem-solving is provided by K. N.:

The intention was to help Gobi consider how best to organise the drinks at break time. The first thing he must consider was what drinks were available; and, if one of his peers wanted a hot drink, was he able to prepare it? Secondly, what was the best way to ask them what they wanted? Some of his friends used signs; some used signs and symbols. Does he know the signs? and does he know how to offer a limited choice to his multiply disabled classmate? Thirdly, how was he going to remember what drinks he had to prepare, and having prepared them, how could he be sure that he gave each person the drinks that they had requested? . . . There is opportunity for Gobi to develop his own strategies to complete the task; however, the teacher would need to be the facilitator, to provide some initial orientation.

From the interactive-process approaches to teaching and learning, the teacher's stance was more respectful of the child's current level of performance. Expectations were raised, children were not seen to require as much external control. Creating environments in which children were encouraged to communicate meant that teachers were less likely to anticipate need; a sure way of disempowering the individual. In a climate of greater interaction, children were seen less as passive recipients and more as active learners, with perhaps greater opportunity to express their own needs and interests. More and more the teacher's behaviour was guided by that of the child.

Houghton et al.'s (1987) research was important here, for they showed that staff working with students with severe disabilities responded at very low rates to student-initiated opportunities of choice or preference. The authors proposed that the heavy tradition of behavioural methodology contributed to this poor response. They write, 'the education of students with severe disabilities is dominated by stimulus control techniques and instructional procedures. Possibly, this heavy emphasis distracts from both observing and responding to student-initiated behaviour, including expressions of choice and preference'.

K. N. acknowledges both the dignity and importance of offering choice-making opportunities to children with severe learning difficulties. She writes:

Choice-making is a valued and intricate part of life. The ability to exercise choice increases personal autonomy and enhances self perception and worth. It provides the foundations upon which children with very severe disabilities develop some control over their environment.

Research into care-giver – infant interaction also influenced teaching approaches within a process model in schools for children with severe learning difficulties, particularly those children at early developmental levels. The work of Stern (1977) and Trevarthen (1977) demonstrated the way in which mothers and fathers attach meaning to early infant behaviours. The Affective Communication Assessment (Coupe et al., 1985) used these principles to enable teachers working with children at pre-intentional levels of communication to interpret their affective responses to various stimuli and place meaning on them; to respond to them as if they are communicative signals. This work has done much to raise teachers' expectations of the potential of pupils at early developmental levels.

Hewett and Nind's (1992) approach to 'intensive interaction' with children with profound learning difficulties draws upon the natural responsiveness of parents to their young infants, and, like the ACA, falls outside the remit of behavioural approaches. It encourages teachers to let the disabled person take the lead: centring upon 'dialogues' of imitation, rhythm, repetition and expectancy (see Nind and Hewett, 1994b).

U. B. offers her interpretation of the Hewett and Nind approach:

1. The learner should be active: students should play an important part in the learning process; they are not empty vessels to be filled passively with knowledge.
2. The learning activity should be fun: learning should be an enjoyable experience, students will wish to continue with a learning activity which gives them pleasure.

3. The learner should share control of the activity with the carer/teacher: students should have some control over how they learn and what they learn. The teacher should provide learning opportunities rather than rigidly controlling outcomes. Like the mother and baby, the teacher should be sensitive to the student's signals so that there is continuous negotiation, even if the child's signals are pre-intentional.

W. I. reports on the effect that Hewett and Nind 'intensive interaction' workshop had on herself and the staff in her school:

Intensive interaction respects the rights, feelings and choices of the student, which I believe is an excellent foundation of any educational approach. The student takes the lead in sessions and these are conducted on his or her terms. When I first started teaching students with severe learning difficulties, I was introduced to behavioural methods. Although I recognised their use in teaching some skills, and I felt it gave me a structure to cling to when I was new to the job, I felt uneasy about teaching communication through behavioural programmes.

. . . I had two students in my class with very severe learning disabilities and challenging behaviour. I tried to develop their language and modify 'unacceptable' behaviour through behavioural techniques. I felt I was fighting a losing battle. I tried to make the students behave in an 'acceptable' and 'age-appropriate' manner. When I sat the children at a table and expected them to 'perform', I had a struggle on my hands. I found I was not respecting the individuals for who they were and what they could do. My sessions lacked fun and excitement. When I heard Dave Hewett speak, I felt inspired. For the first time my intuitive feelings about teaching were reflected in an educational approach. 'Intensive interaction' gave me the structure, the principles and the strategies to work with children in ways in which I could believe in . . .

My classroom teaching began to change. I allowed all the students more control over their own learning and lives. When students displayed challenging behaviour I tried to view it as a communicative act rather than responding in a punitive manner. For example, Timothy regularly threw tantrums when we played whole group turn-taking games or had our class meeting (a forum for students to discuss issues raised by themselves and chaired by a student). Previously, I had applied 'time-out' unsuccessfully. But now I began to view the behaviour as a message saying, 'I can't cope with this, I don't want to be here'. . .

While respecting the chronological age of the students, I placed my emphasis upon 'person-appropriate' rather than strictly 'age-appropriate' expectations. For instance, one boy at an early developmental level loved to play with dolls, by himself. He became very agitated when these were removed from him and replaced with more 'appropriate' toys. I reasoned that he needed the dolls for security as well as the pleasure they gave him (there seemed to be very few things in his life that gave him pleasure and that he could enjoy independently). In class, I gave him a box of dolls and puppets representing different ages, teenagers, grandparents, mums and dads. He was extremely happy with them, I would argue that his behaviour, in consequence became much more 'age-appropriate' when they were not removed.

W. I. describes the effect that 'intensive interaction' had on one student taught by another member of staff and her own experiences of how the improvements were generalised in other settings:

Sally is an eighteen year-old woman. She is pre-verbal and has many stereotypical behaviours, for example, spinning round and around and holding any object she could find in front of her face. Sarah carried out self-injurious behaviour, for instance tearing her hair out. She could not make her needs known and did not relate to the other students and very rarely to staff. During the interaction sessions, the teacher kept very close. She followed what she did, moved around the room with her, lying down when she lay down and imitated her vocalisations. After two terms, Sally made progress in sociability and communication. She displays pleasure during her sessions, her concentration span has increased, and she has a more relaxed manner. This is demonstrated by the fact that Sally now approaches the teacher when the sessions begin. She shows pleasure when the teacher makes the same noises as her. When her hand is caressed, she places her hand on the teacher as a signal to continue. Sally can now work intensively with her teacher for up to ten minutes. Her increased sociability has spilled over into other areas. For example, during a multisensory massage session, she spontaneously came up to me and started vocalising. When I copied her, she smiled. On another occasion, Sally came and sat on my lap and put my arms around her. Before intensive interaction was used with her, Sally would tolerate very little physical contact and I had no records of her initiating it.

In the descriptions above, we can see the reciprocity and bonding that Stern, Trevarthen, and others decribed in their observations of natural parent-child interactions. We can also see Schaffer's (1977) assertion that learning must first have a strong social context before it can be internalised in the individual. K. N. writes:

For Schaffer, the immediate care-giver's relationships form the first crucial step in the process of socialisation. Early sequences of interaction normally develop via the infant's own spontaneous behaviour which is repeated and elaborated upon by the parent, so that the idea of the two way flow of communication is set in motion. Schaffer states that mothers tend to interpret the child's interactions and give them meaning and intent, following the child's lead, even when such interactions may not be intentional.

K. N. first describes a student with very severe disabilities and how theory of child development informs her practice using early care-giver child routines:

Stuart is a student with profound and multiple learning difficulties. His severe learning difficulties are compounded by additional physical and visual handicaps. Stuart has cerebral palsy, a dislocated right hip and wears a body jacket for a forward curvature of the spine. He is non-ambulant and is dependent upon a wheelchair. He has some control over the movement of his head. He can lift it up and move it to either side. He can lift his left arm up to above shoulder level and can bring it towards his midline to clap. His right arm has far less movement. When excited, Stuart can move his legs in a kicking movement. He has hydrocephalus which is controlled by two shunts, only one of which is working. Such complications resulted in Stuart being registered blind three years ago. He is also epileptic.

Stuart has a keen sense of hearing and enjoys contact with adults, particularly if this involves action songs, coughing, sneezing, general turn-taking routines and music. With the latter, his bodily movements suggest he is able to discriminate favourite tunes.

K. N. uses her knowledge of language and communication to select appropriate assessments and then plan an intervention programme to promote choice-making:

Communication is seen as being concerned with ways in which the individual intentionally influences the behaviour of others. Language is seen as a way in which the individual internalises and codes aspects of experience (Kiernan, 1987). They are essentially different when considering children at early development levels. The student with pmld may well be able to communicate before he or she has recognisable language skills. This will inevitably be through non-verbal means, e.g., gestures, eye-pointing, pushing things away, pulling, pointing, vocalising, crying, etc.

The full PVCS (Kiernan and Reid, 1987) was completed on Stuart, with the assistance of those people who knew Stuart best, his teachers, assistants, and key worker from his residential home . . . The ACA (Coupe et al., 1987) was used to help me further in planning a teaching programme. This gave me the structure by which to observe in greater detail Stuart's affective behaviours.

K. N. uses this information to formulate a strengths and needs chart.

Strengths	Needs
Stuart has a relatively high level of social awareness. He likes being with people and demonstrates a great interest in people.	Stuart needs to be given opportunities for choice-making; he has not learned that he can communicate his needs and interests (and satisfy them) by influencing the behaviour of other people. Stuart needs to be taught ways of attaining need satisfaction and negation, i.e., the adults around him need to interpret and respond to his emotional expressions as communicative acts.
Stuart has good hearing and good listening skills.	Encourage Stuart to locate source of sound. Use audible clues, e.g., splashing drinks in cup at 'drinks time' to build up anticipation and predictability.
Stuart enjoys physical interaction.	Stuart is blind and therefore needs physical help to explore his environment. He would benefit from a range of turn-taking routines, and tension-expectancy games routines (see Nind & Hewett, 1994).
Stuart makes spontaneous vocalisations.	Use voice-activated toys and computer programmes to build up understanding of cause and effect.

CONCLUSION

This chapter has looked at two approaches to teaching and learning; the behavioural and interactive approaches. Traditional behavioural approaches will always have a place in special education. It would be a rash person who claimed that it would not be worth trying a behavioural approach to teaching a profoundly disabled child to visually track, for example. It would be a mistake to think that, in practice, behavioural and process approaches are mutually exclusive (see Farrell, 1992). K. N. states that it is possible to be 'interactive when adopting a behavioural approach, and utilise behavioural principles when working within an interactive model'. It is a little like the reading debate – should we use a phonic approach or encourage children to look for meaning by guessing? etc. In reality, teachers use the best from both (or indeed all possible) approaches.

Special education has certainly moved on since the 1970s (even taking into account the major stumbling block in the late 1980s). The interactive approach, particularly in relation to language and communication, has been driven by a strong research base. This approach has done much to reorientate teachers' attention from focusing on what children cannot do, to giving them more control over what they can do.

A final point which ends on a note of optimism, and yet offers special educators a challenge is expressed in Staff of Rectory Paddock School (op. cit.):

(We are confronted with) the need not only to make the child as competent as possible in certain skills, but also to make him aware of how those skills can be used by him, to what extent and in what circumstances they can help him, – also in what circumstances they can *not* help him and some other information-gathering strategy must be employed. (original italics)

In other words, in addition to skills in cognition and language, children need 'metacognitive' and 'metalinguistic' skills, i.e., within the limits of their awareness, they can see the use of applying their knowledge and awareness to 'real-life'.

Now that the impact of the National Curriculum is beginning to wear off, it is time for special educators to meet this challenge and continue to develop new approaches to teaching children with severe learning difficulties.

7

Teachers, Number Work and Reading

The Warnock Report (1978) recommended that there should be closer links between special and mainstream schools. This was in terms of the three levels of integration described in the Report (social, locational and functional) and in terms of what schools can learn from each other's curriculum practice. Of course, the two are closely linked. Special school teachers accompanying children integrating into the mainstream classroom are bound to bring with them specific skills. This chapter is about how mainstream teachers can learn from what teachers do in special schools. Since the publication of the Code of Practice, teachers will be increasingly preoccupied with IEPs. In special education, teachers and IEPs go back a long way. This chapter looks at what special school teachers are doing in literacy and number work. Despite the recommendations of Warnock, there appears to be little partnership between mainstream and special school teachers. The extracts below demonstrate examples of good practice. We can all learn from them, wherever we teach. Good curriculum practice is context free.

One of the authors (V. H.), teaching in a school for children with severe learning difficulties in the 1980s, remembers getting increasingly involved with a eight year-old child attending a mainstream school. David was a statemented child with very poor reading skills. V. H. met David while he and members of his class joined the mainstream class for one afternoon a week during integrated sessions. V. H. often found himself gravitating towards this child, who seemed to have good language skills, yet to all intents and purposes, was a poorer reader than some of the children with severe learning difficulties. At the time, the children were working on a topic on 'ourselves' (all good topics stand the test of time!). The special school children were paired with the mainstream children to learn about their families, friends, etc. David was working with a Down's boy called Alex. Alex had taken in his symbol reading book about a recent school journey, and he was reading this book to David. This book was a personalised reading book containing photographs and short sentences, with Makaton symbols written under the text. The special school child, Alex, used Makaton signs to accompany his speech and was using Makaton symbols as a bridge to learning traditional orthography. Alex read to David using signs to supplement his poor articulation.

The two children were engrossed in this reading book. David read the symbol reading book back to Alex and with the encouragement of the classroom teacher, they both drew a picture of the sea front at Westgate, the setting of Alex's holiday.

After the integrated session, David's teacher made an appointment to visit one of the reading sessions in the special school to see how symbols were used in the reading process. What follows is somewhat predictable; however, it was not the use of symbols which David's teacher imported back into the mainstream classroom. It was the individualised approach, the use of photographs, the way teachers in the special schools encouraged the children to 'bring their oral language competence to bear on reading' (Donaldson and Reid, 1982) by using personalised reading books. In the special school, with the emerging readers, the teachers used a language experience approach (as used in Breakthrough to Literacy) where, in response to a stimulus, e.g., an illustration or photograph, the children make up the text themselves. They did this to ensure that the text made immediate sense to the reader, that the text reflected the child's linguistic ability and to instil in the children confidence, to provide them with opportunities to predict unfamiliar words according to the meaning of the sentence.

David's teacher took on board these approaches. It was time consuming; the teacher had to find time to make personalised reading books for David. However, as his language was not delayed, he made rapid progress. Using his first few personalised reading books, David quickly learned to read for meaning as the text centred upon his world and represented the kind of language that he used. Finally, he seemed to understand the purpose of print and over subsequent visits to the school, the author saw that he was quickly weaned off personalised books on to real books and commercial reading schemes.

This is a real example from the author's experience of how dissemination of special school practice can inform teaching and learning in the mainstream context. Teaching and learning in special education can be such an insular practice. One hopes that further integration of special school children into the mainstream classroom may bring teachers in both settings closer together. The rest of this chapter is devoted to what special school and mainstream teachers are doing to meet the needs of individual children in number and literacy. There is much to be learned from them by all of us.

TEACHING CHILDREN TO READ

K. N. states that teachers of children with special needs have to be very clear about what is involved in the reading process:

The Education Reform Act puts pressure on those working with severe learning difficulties to teach them to read. To take on board the implications of this for the wide range of ability in special schools, teachers need to be clear about the processes involved in learning to read, and to focus in particular on the problems which a child with severe learning difficulties may face, e.g., their developmental delay in language. It is acknowledged that written language is very different from spoken language, but to teach children to read, links between the two need to be made. Previous notions that the process of understanding written language is essentially the same as understanding spoken language of the written language have been rejected. Donaldson (1989) writes, 'if this were the case then written language would also have to arise spontaneously in the course of other shared activities, with all the give and take and immediacy of speech. Written language is not used in this way.' (p. 12)

K.N. continues:

Vygotsky (1966) was also quite clear about the distinction between the two: 'Written speech is a separate linguistic function differing from oral speech in both structure and mode of functioning'. Although written language is not acquired in the same way as spoken language, children's awareness that there is a link between the two needs to be developed. Reid (1983) suggests ways in which this can be done. Firstly, shared reading helps the early reader understand the purpose of print, that marks on the page carry meaning. Shared reading, where most of the time, the adult does the reading for the child, but where the teacher draws the child's attention to certain features of the reading process, e.g., the intonation of voice when reading dialogue, pointing to words, pictures, etc. 'Big Books' with familiar text can be useful here, when groups of children can be encouraged to predict and join in.

Another useful strategy to help children with special needs develop reading skills, especially appropriate for children who find it difficult to write, is to provide them with sets of printed words, e.g., 'Breakthrough to Literacy'. Children can be encouraged to put the words together to make simple sentences. A child whom I shall call Victoria, treasured her folder of words and with practice would arrange them to make meaningful sentences and then draw pictures to accompany them. From this, the teacher helped her to make her own individual book using a concept keyboard. She proudly put this book in the bookcase with all the other books for her peers to read. Sequencing words in this way seemed to raise Victoria's awareness of language, for example, word order, word endings, -ed, -s and -ing.

The third way that Reid talks about making links between spoken and written language is developing children's awareness of what Donaldson (1989) calls 'embedded' print. Here, written language, like spoken language, benefits from the support of a non-linguistic context. Examples of embedded print are the words that surround us in the environment, e.g., words on tins of food, words in shopping aisles in supermarkets, etc. Drawing children's attention to embedded print makes explicit the purpose of print, i.e., words carry meaning. Embedded print can be used in the classroom, not just in the teaching of social sight vocabulary, but in labels on storage containers, labels on cupboards, the sort of labelling which serves a real communicative function.

There is another important distinction between written language and spoken language:

Teachers should be aware that written language is structurally different from speech, and is not speech written down (Donaldson, 1989). What may be represented in written form in books, we may not say in the course of everyday conversation. In children's literature, there is often what Donaldson calls the 'rich and complex' language of books, this language, especially for the child with severe learning difficulties, may be an unfamiliar language. Hinchcliffe (1991) proposes that for children with severe learning difficulties, who are beginning to learn to read, the teacher should ensure that the 'written language represents the kind of spoken language that they can understand; it seems pointless to confront them in print with language which they could not understand even in speech'. (p. 26)

K. N. recognises the value, at least in the early stage of learning to read, of providing children with personalised reading material. She writes:

The advantage of using 'home-made' books is that it can begin where the child is. If the teacher uses the child's language as the basis of the text it can demonstrate directly to the child the transformation of speech into writing. It sets written language within a meaningful context and enables the text to be individually tailored to the linguistic level of the child. Donaldson (op cit.) encourages us to do this. She states that 'whatever we do, we should respect the individuality of the children we teach. Even if a way of teaching is good for the many, some may fail to thrive on it. When this becomes apparent, other ways should always be tried'. (p. 31)

These essential principles underlying K. N.'s highly differentiated approach to teaching reading to children with severe learning difficulties have great application to intervention in mainstream schools; however, in the special school context, more favourable staff to child ratio makes such differentiation, in terms of preparation of materials and one to one teaching makes the teacher's life much easier.

Y. J., who teaches in a secondary school for students with severe learning difficulties, writes about involvement of all children, regardless of ability in the reading process:

There are many students, particularly in the upper school, who are learning to read 'functional, social-sight vocabulary' – some of whom have been doing this for years. They are able to read words such as 'pay here', 'toilet', 'way out', etc. It is possible that some of these students, particularly those who have good language skills, could have learned to read more than just isolated words if they had been given the appropriate opportunities. Children in mainstream schools are expected to read. Reading is regarded as a priority and is seen as a 'measure' for good teaching. There are stages that young children are seen to go through; everyone expects mainstream children to learn, nobody really gives up. This is not the case in schools for children with severe learning difficulties, where disability and priorities are different, justifiably so. Gurney (1976) quotes Bateman (1965) as stating that 'children who have learning disorders are those who manifest an educationally significant discrepancy between their estimated intellectual potential and the actual level of performance related to basic disorders in the learning process'. As educational gaps widen with age, it becomes the 'learning disorder' to blame, not the teaching process. In terms of teaching reading, teachers can easily give up; the children's difficulties in this area mean that the whole teaching process can stagnate, be more prolonged and appear less relevant. For these children, failure or slow progress in reading is often explained in terms of their disability rather than on poor teaching. Teachers' expectations of children's performance can be unduly pessimistic.

For the reasons explored earlier, most children with severe learning difficulties also experience great difficulty in learning to read. Teachers are often faced with the dilemma of whether to spend valuable curricular time on continuing to help them develop reading skills. Some children's learning difficulties may be sufficiently severe for the teacher to abandon all efforts of trying to teach them to read, and in some cases, for example children with profound and multiple learning difficulties, this decision would appear to be justified. But even for the more able students, is the time and effort teaching them to read worthwhile when the outcomes are often so limited? Few of them will leave school with a reading age of more than about eight years. One of the authors (V. H.) has argued elsewhere that these arguments may unnecessarily restrict the learning opportunities of children with severe learning difficulties. Reading ages concern only the products of our intervention; they cannot measure the processes that learning to read can afford the child, even at a rudimentary level (Hinchcliffe, 1991). It also depends what we mean by reading. Reading is not just an independent activity; only older children and adults 'bury themselves in books'. Children's first introduction to text is usually set within rich participant social contexts; on their parents' knees children learn about people, narrative and culture. Learning to read is not a solitary activity, it is interactive, probably the best example of a learning process which progresses from the social to the individual, from the inter-psychological to the intra-psychological (Vygotsky, 1934). When the child of one of the authors was approaching two years of age, she became transfixed when she saw a bee in the garden, probably for the first time. When it finally flew away, she took her father by the hand and mysteriously led him into the house. She stopped below some bookshelves, pointed towards the books and looked at him, intently. She wanted him to find a book and read to her about bees. Even at this young age, she had some understanding about the purpose of reading, what books are for, and about the pleasures that they can afford.

To develop this rudimentary awareness of reading, among severely learning disabled youngsters, would seem to be an honourable intention. For those pupils who, after our efforts, do not become independent readers, such understanding may encourage them still to participate in the reading process, even if they remain dependent upon more skilled readers.

Y.J . writes about the dangers of placing a ceiling on children's development:

By denying children the opportunity to develop reading skills, apart from depriving them of pleasure, there is also denial of a wealth of learning opportunities and experiences availed only to the literate. Even with the most basic of skills, the person with severe learning difficulties can function with greater autonomy, independence and dignity. It permits greater interaction with the environment, greater confidence in the community, e.g., while travelling, shopping and using everyday services. Literacy is an important part of daily life.

Y. J. continues by describing a highly individualised approach to teaching reading to a student with Down's Syndrome. The teacher builds on the student's knowledge of Makaton signs and symbols and teaches her to 'symbol read' as a bridge to reading traditional orthography. Y. J. uses a similar 'language experience' approach described by K. N., above. She also begins by using personalised reading books and photographs to ensure that the text is within the student's experience:

Mary is able to follow instructions at the 5 word level on the Derbyshire Language Scheme. She has an extensive repertoire of Makaton signs and recognises a great number of Makaton symbols. She is able to use her signs to express herself at the 2–3 word level. Initially, Makaton symbols were used in personalised reading books containing photographs of Mary and her friends involved in familiar activities. To begin with the text describing the picture or photograph consisted of only 2 symbol/word phrases (words were written below the symbols), most of them subject-verb constructions (Tom's drinking). But soon, subject verb-object combinations were introduced (Mum's kicking ball). The teacher would sign key words and speak in normal, grammatical English and Mary would be encouraged to sign and speak.

Y. J. describes the success of this method in teaching Mary literacy skills. Mary continued to use signs, symbols and speech in the following scheme of work:

Expressive language	Receptive language	Auditory & visual memory
Selective indiv. symbol cards to describe pictures/photos.	Manipulating 'Derbyshire' objects in response to reading symbol instruction cards.	Matching symbol card to signed/spoken instruction.
Pressing symbols on concept keyboard overlay to describe pictures/photos.	Matching symbol sentences to photos & pictures.	

Makaton Symbols

Representation	Functional skills	Symbol reading
Drawing pictures to symbol sentences.	Cooking using symbol recipe cards.	Reading personalised symbol books.
		Organising school timetable using symbols.

A. A. also utilised Makaton symbols in the construction of flash cards to teach language and literacy to children with SLD:

I have always found that [these children] have great difficulty in putting their own thoughts down in writing. This is a very complex task requiring several different operations being performed in a correct sequence, and some tasks being performed simultaneously, i.e.,

• Deciding on the content or subject of the sentence or phrase;
• Composing the sentence or phrase, mentally choosing and sequencing the words;
• Remembering the whole phrase until it has all been written down (children find this particularly difficult because as they concentrate on the spelling of each word and the formation of each letter, they often forget the other words to be written);
• Writing each word in the correct sequence;
• Spelling each word correctly, identifying and sequencing letters;
• Forming the shape of each letter correctly.

This resource uses a range of double-sided flash cards, each card carries one word. On one side of the card appears the word and a picture, and on the reverse side the makaton symbol. This becomes an easy to use library linking signs and symbols. The flash cards are displayed alphabetically on a board screwed to the classroom wall (Figures 5 and 6). The board is divided into four sections: naming words (nouns), doing words (verbs), describing words (adjectives) and other words.

I have found that it is particularly useful in developing literacy work as with only a small amount of adult support it enables children to put their own thoughts down in writing. A story, group discussion or news-time will act as the stimulus, encouraging a child to give a sentence or phrase depending on the child's individual stage of development. Knowledge of the child's expressive word level on the Derbyshire Language scheme enables the adult to establish the complexity of sentence one can expect from a child.

The child or supporting adult can then select from the display board the two, three or four important words needed to make up the sentence or phrase. The child may then be able to sequence the symbols in the correct order. Depending on the child's level of language, the linking words 'in', 'on', 'the', can be left out or included.

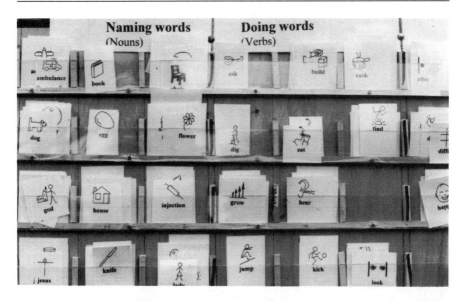

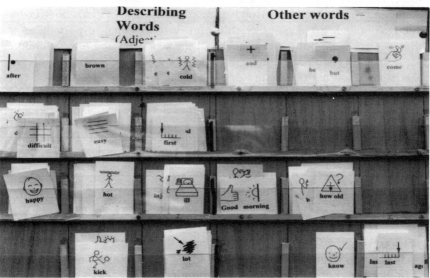

Figures 5 and 6   A 'library' of flash cards

The child then takes the cards to the school office and photocopies them in sequence, to get a permanent print-out of the sentence. At this stage the adult can add, if appropriate, any of the linking words. The child can then either copy the writing beneath the printed words, or an adult can write out the sentence again for the child to trace over.

Encouraged by their success children are often motivated to read and re-read their own work and make up further new sentences. This method of developing writing skills has been particularly valuable when children compose their own stories.

This approach echoes that often used in nursery and infant classes with emergent writers; what is different is the detailed exposition of the actual significance of the signs and symbols which are ultimately recognised as writing. As in so much of the work with children with SLD, it works by making visible the teaching and learning process.

J. P., supporting a group of three eight year-old children in a mainstream primary school, describes a highly differentiated approach to teaching AT1-AT5 in English Key Stage 2. The three children were referred to the Literacy Support Service in which she works because they were seen to be seriously underachieving. Before she describes her intervention, she talks about the constraints placed upon her time:

I was constrained by time on two levels: firstly, I was only in school twice a week: Monday afternoons and Friday mornings. Secondly, my designated time blocks were sub-divided into three sessions to accommodate three groups of children. It was therefore extremely difficult to collaborate with their class teacher and work together. Liaison was more or less restricted to coffee breaks. Although limited, these times of collusion were essential, especially as the children were aware of them. I looked at the work that these three children were doing and I compared it with the work of the rest of the class. In this way, I was able to see the continuum of ability in the class, and where my three children were placed. The range of ability was enormous. Children's reading ages ranged from ten years down to my three children, who could be described as emergent readers, with a reading age of about five years. The gap between spelling ages seemed just as wide. Quite a few of the children could write in neat, cursive script, whereas my children's handwriting was irregular and often illegible.

The following extracts show J. P.'s assessment and intervention for these three children:

AT1: Speaking and Listening
It soon became clear to me that all three of the children experienced difficulty responding appropriately to a range of more complex instructions (level 2). I administered the Quest Diagnostic Reading Profile Test and this highlighted auditory sequential memory weaknesses. The test is simple; you say four unrelated things and the pupil has to repeat them in the same sequence. You do the same with numbers. This pinpointed one of the problems faced by their teacher, namely that these boys were never really ready to begin with everyone else in the group; they were 'unfocused', and often needed instructions to be repeated and clarified. Several things could be done immediately to improve their memory. I worked on oral instructions: I would give them two things to do and ask them to repeat them back to me before beginning the tasks. Sometimes,

I would give them a sequence of things to do without referring them back to me for repetition. This was extended to a sequence of three or more things to remember. Another useful memory game is 'Granny went shopping and in her basket she put . . .' At each person's turn, another item is added to the list. Items must be repeated in the same sequence.

T. was very good at describing events, but not so good at listening. P. lost concentration easily when one of the others was talking. John would interrupt – not only the others, but even himself.

. . . The advantage of working in a small group was that I could mark their written work with them present and discuss it with them. This individual evaluation focused them and gave them time to explain themselves more fully. This rarely happened in class.

AT2: Reading

With this group, a good starting point seemed to be knowledge of the alphabet referred to in item (e) 'demonstrate knowledge of the alphabet in using word books and simple dictionaries'. The word attack skills section of 'Quest' showed weaknesses in all three children in letter-recognition, sight vocabulary, simple blends, beginnings and endings, digraphs, the silent 'e' rule and reversals. For these children, the foundation stones for successful reading appeared not to be in place.

I think it is important to use letters made of plastic or wood which you can pick up and move around. I used my set of Galt letters. The children learned to sequence the alphabet. They were taught to lay out the letters in the shape of a rainbow so that they could see the alphabet as a whole. Removing two or three letters while their backs were turned is a good game to reinforce the sequence and help them identify the letters with their letter sounds. When the children were confident in naming each letter of the alphabet, we moved on to learning the vowels and understanding their importance in words. This was important because they often wrote words without vowels, e.g., 'drk' for 'dark'. Using their Galt letters, they removed the vowels and set them out in a column. Then they would use the vowels to try and make as many words as they could from the remaining letters. Then they were helped to make sentences using these words. A further development was to dictate these sentences back to them and encourage them to write them from memory. This seemed to help them visualise the words for recall.

Using the Galt letters, we did some more work on auditory sequential memory. I said three letters, the child had to repeat them in the same order and then take them out of their alphabet rainbow. As they became better at this, I increased the number of letters in the sequence and used letters which sound similar, e.g., b d, m n, i y.

I used letter tracking exercises to improve directionality. We then went on to tracking high frequency words using Mcnally's list of 200 most used words. I gave the children two target words and they had to find them among the other words. They were encouraged to run a felt-tip pen along the line, beneath the words, drawing a ring around the target words as they found them. Speed is the essence, so I used a stop-watch to time them.

Sequencing is an important pre-requisite to reading fluently. Sometimes, I would copy out and cut up a sentence from their reader and ask them to put the words together. I would draw their attention to demarcation points, e.g., capital letters and full-stops.

Their reading was, of course, full of inaccuracies. I had to find ways of getting them to re-read text to look for meaning. At the end of a short passage, I would ask them to find a word or a group of words. I also used to spend time discussing the story with the children. It often struck me how little they really understood of the story. P. read in such a monotonous fashion; his intonation of voice communicated that he felt reading was a pointless chore. I tried to teach him to 'gather' small words quickly, e.g., 'he went into the . . .' and, 'she saw a big . . .' I wanted to help him to use voice inflexion, and see the link between reading and speaking.

AT3: Writing

I decided that the children's writing work should be brief and related to their current experience both at home and at school. J. often found it difficult to begin a piece of written work. I wanted to teach him that ideas are often only released after the pen has been put to paper. I often wrote alongside him. I stressed that crossing out was allowed – first drafts were not to be viewed as perfect. It was the ideas that were important; we were less concerned with spelling. Eventually they got the hang of it and we had fun hearing each other's stories.

Freeing them to write was one thing, but getting them to look critically at the end result was much more difficult. I wanted them to get into the habit of reading carefully what they had written to see if they had written what they had intended to write. These children made no real attempt to proof-read their work because they were not clear in their minds what they were looking for. They had become passive about having their work marked, and corrected. Initially, I just wanted them to read their work and put in capital letters and full-stops. Then I encouraged them to read their sentences to see if they made sense. As a double check, they read each other's work. We talked about why it is easier to spot someone else's errors than our own. We also proof-read some text printed from the 'Alpha to Omega Workbook'. They enjoyed doing this. I had told them that this was a skilled job, mainly done by teachers.

AT4: Spelling

The Daniel's and Diack spelling test revealed the children's weaknesses in some initial letter sounds, blends and vowel digraphs. I provided the children with a slim word notebook which was to be their spelling record. Their parents were involved in short tests. Any word which had three ticks next to it was considered learned and crossed off the list. The main aim was to give them confidence and a sense of achievement. The children took pride in their notebooks which soon filled up with words and stickers. I showed them how to use the 'look, say, cover, write, check' method. Each word would get this treatment three times. To help them develop a visual image of the word, they immediately wrote it with their eyes shut.

AT5: Handwriting

J. and T. were at level 1. P.'s handwriting was legible, but he reversed the letters b, d and p. J.'s writing suffered from his 'strangle-hold' grip. I gave him a rubber pencil-grip and this helped him enormously. T.'s poor handwriting was in part due to his desk position. The way he squared up to the table gave him a very unnatural, cramped sitting position. I insisted that he assumed a more upright posture and encouraging him to slant his paper to the right and to use his left hand to steady the paper. The spelling practice seemed to contribute to better handwriting. The repetition of writing the same word seemed to help.

The intervention described above may be considered as a 'back to basics' approach to improving children's literacy skills. J. P.'s work and the work of the other teachers before her demonstrate how teachers use both meaning-centred and code-centred strategies to help children learn to read; what Smith calls the 'inside-out' and 'outside-in' approaches, respectively (Smith, 1978, 1986).

NUMBER

Z. R., working with children in a school for mainly autistic children, describes a painstaking programme of work in mathematics based on detailed observation and a highly differentiated approach. Z. R. uses Gillham's Basic Number Diagnostic Test (Gillham, 1990) to plan work for a small group of children. He writes:

In a general sense perhaps the main objective was to provide some interesting and enjoyable tasks and activities in maths: some of the children in the group (as well as others in the school as a whole) had been experiencing some failure with number work. I aimed for some activities which would capture their attention and which hopefully would not be threatening or seemingly too difficult but would also be challenging and stimulating. I wanted to guard against the idea of being right or wrong and to enlarge their experience away from a work-book model of pages of sums just being marked with a cross or a tick. For Darren and Jim the higher achievers I hoped to plan some work which would extend their experience and challenge them. From this I hoped to investigate how (and if) the children were thinking, how they use numbers and manipulate materials; do they think about the problem; do they have any system of partic-ular strategies? It was also hoped that over the course of the project maths would be brought into everyday situations and other activities; in music, creative work, and as the project took place during the second half of the autumn term maths would also be found and exploited in the Christmas theme. It was intended that the children would all gain in a variety of ways from the

Figures 7–10   Helping with numbers

experiences offered. They would have practice in the recognition of numerals; they would be able to perform simple operations e.g. + and – to 10 and the more able children would be able to explore addition and pattern in number. They would all be able to record their activity to some extent.

The categories making up the test seemed to provide a core on which to build a short programme of work and activities to present to the children. The activities together with some examples of the pupils' responses are given below.

Reciting numbers
At the beginning of the first sessions the children were asked simply to count as far as they could in the same way as that asked in the test. Dan made several attempts but always found difficulty going on from 10 whilst Darren and Jim were quite able to continue counting at least to 100 and further. The two able boys enjoyed thinking up counting songs and action rhymes they knew: 'One two three four five, once I caught a fish alive', and 'Five currant buns'. Towards the end of the period approaching Christmas we sang the Caribbean version of 'The twelve days of Christmas' which formed part of the half term's work leading to the Christmas celebration. With my own class, we did the display and the whole school learned the song. This was an enjoyable experience, giving them practice with numbers greater than 10 and counting forwards and backwards.

Naming numbers
We chose books from the class library e.g. 'The Hungry Caterpillar'; I wrote numbers on flash cards or paper and asked the children to 'read' them. Numbers were written on an A3 Matrix, firstly by me and the children were asked to point to each number in turn and try to name it. In another session they copied my numbers in sequences 1 to 5 recording this on large sheets of paper or below my numbers on the matrix.

Copying over
The A3 Matrix contained four boxes of numbers 1 2 3 in dotted outlines; Dan and Tim were asked to copy over the numbers, joining two dots. I provided a starting point with a large 'dot'; Dan needed help with focusing on the starting point and controlling the pen but seemed to show a slight improvement in fine motor control with practice.

Copying underneath
A similar A3 sheet was provided with my numbers written in the boxes: Dan, Tim and Stephen all practised writing the numbers below my number shapes. Dan could not do this without dotted number shapes. Tim and Stephen managed very well and over the time available practised numbers 1 to 7. To help Dan develop his concept of the shape of a number, we cut out some large numerals 1 to 5 from some textured plastic material collected from the scrap bins. He was invited to trace over the numbers with his fingers and then experiment with the shapes to see if he could recognise the numbers and place them in the correct sequence.

Counting bricks

We used a variety of objects for counting unifix cubes, wooden blocks, cotton reels, beads. Dan and Tim were quite successful with this and having 'concrete' materials to handle were sufficiently well motivated to continue the activity for up to 30 minutes. On one occasion when I went into the classroom two of the boys were sitting on the floor building lego models; they counted numbers of wheels on the vehicles they made; they tried estimating the number of red or blue bricks contained in their models.

Addition and subtraction

Set diagrams on A3 sheets were provided; we explored a variety of ways to do simple addition. To begin with some placed unifix cubes in the circles and counted them all together to arrive at a total. Others were able to write a number in each circle and write the answer to their sum. Other objects were placed in the circles: pencils, counters, cotton reels. To extend the activity after the children had had practice manipulating materials, I asked them to do a sum in their heads; this was enjoyable and they came up with a variety of answers – some were guessing, others e.g. Jim and Darren could do this with accuracy.

Additional activities

It became clear that Dan was having the most difficulty and needed more early work to develop his ability to recognise numbers and to count with bricks or other objects. Although the diagnostic test showed up some of his difficulties I felt that it provided perhaps a narrow view; I decided to carry out some of the activities contained in the Mathsteps programme (LDA). This is a developmental programme of maths activities which contains a certain amount of built in assessment and pointers towards remediation. With Dan I was able to work through a series of activities from the number section of the programme; a selection of the items were explored; at the initial level the pupil is asked simply to imitate the teacher by selecting a small number of coloured reels. Following activities gave practice in counting and sequencing reels, counters or blocks. We followed the instructions given on the work cards; Dan counted out piles of reels according to colour and made taller or shorter piles of the objects.

One item in Mathsteps gives children practice in writing number symbols 1 to 5. Tim and Stephen both spent a little time doing this activity producing legible though not always correctly formed numbers.

The pyramid activity

Jim and Darren stacked large plastic bricks, writing numbers 1 2 3 4 on the first layer. Jim and Darren easily did the additions for each consecutive layer sometimes using fingers or unifix cubes to check their results. Over a short session they tried three different sequences of numbers on the first layer of bricks: 1,2,3,4, 4,3,2,1, 4,2,3,1. Each of these sequences totalled 20 on the top brick.

Figure 11　Using bricks to help with number sequences

Calendars and number games

As part of their work on the Christmas theme, the children had made an advent calendar; this provided a stimulus for practice with counting and sequencing.

A variety of games were used. The children played dice games, some using dotted dice, others using numbered dice. Darren brought a small pinball machine to school which he shared with the other children. They all enjoyed these activities and games such as snakes and ladders, Ludo and the Hat game. The children responded well to having me in their classroom, looking forward to my next visit. Stephen wanted to work with me every time I came into the room! He would come over and ask: 'my turn today?' Tim often said whose turn is it today Chris? Is it me? I had to find ways to explain that sometimes I wanted to work with someone else!

As the activities progressed; I was able to assess the obvious individual differences in the way the children responded and could then modify the activities as we went along. Some of my notes were useful for the class teacher to include in the children's record books. The two more able children, Darren and Jim, very much enjoyed doing the pyramid activity and I think their interest and involvement shows in the accompanying photographs. This activity continued for almost an hour; a lengthy time for children who may have difficulty concentrating or persevering with a task. Darren is usually a quiet boy who says little; in the beginning he seemed reluctant to join in but once he got going his interest was aroused and he proved to be a good worker. Stephen is usually very active, sitting still for longer than a few minutes at a time was very difficult for him but I was very pleased with his response. He worked through the diagnostic test without interruption and he concentrated well on counting and making sets of the cubes.

On another occasion when practising writing numerals Tim noticed that Dan was having some difficulty: he took Dan's hand to help him form the numbers. Tim was delightfully keen to do the work and he enjoyed the challenges: he copied my numbers 5, 6, 7 underneath several times and then wanted to do it on his own on a blank sheet. He said 'don't wanna see it, Z'. He made some very legible attempts at writing the numbers and I felt he had really benefited from the experience.

A. A., working in a school for children with SLD, has developed a finely tuned assessment of children's counting errors:

Number and an understanding of counting are basic skills essential to effective everyday living. As adults we may forget the complexity of learning some of our basic numeracy, and observations of young children in a mainstream nursery show how quickly children develop an understanding of numeracy.

Working with children with SLD one begins to appreciate some of the difficulties that these children have in understanding number skills. To count and understand number one must first master several skills. Generally children begin by counting by rote, 'one, two, three, four' (ordinal). Though this in itself is not a mathematical skill, it is necessary for further number development. Good practice effects an environment where counting by rote is introduced incidentally within everyday activities. As a child climbs the ladder of a slide an adult might say One, Two Three, etc. Conversely children can be introduced to numeracy by experiencing cardinal numbers: 'This is two' *(XX)*, 'this is three' *(XXX)*. Children can be helped to gain a full understanding of number by experiencing both ordinal and cardinal values.

Children initially need the support of objects to help them with an understanding of number: this is known as *concrete understanding*. A full comprehension of numeracy comes when one can demonstrate an understanding without the need of objects or props, this is known as *abstract understanding*. It is this abstract understanding that many children with SLD find difficult, or even impossible.

An analysis of numeracy shows that there are five basic rules in counting. Though important, in a survey of 20 primary school teachers the author found that 15 were not aware of them. He has also found that a knowledge of these rules has helped in analysing what areas of number a child has grasped and where their knowledge was still lacking. These five rules of counting are:

1. One to one. Each item to be counted is given one, and only one, tag or name.

2. Stable order. The list of tags is always recited in the same order.
3. Cardinality. The last tag in an array indicates the size of the set.
4. Abstraction. The first three rules can be used to count and group or set.
5. Order – irrelevance. Any group or items can be tagged in any order as long as each is only tagged once. This final rule separates counting from just labelling. (Buckley & Bird, 1994)

As children begin to develop counting skills their concrete understanding is aided by the fact that they pick up, touch, or point to objects. This pointing task is an important yet difficult process. Counting is a complicated activity. A child has to co-ordinate two separate activities, whilst at the same time making a correct utterance, or saying the appropriate counting word. The two activities are: Pointing-object co-ordination, and Pointing-word co-ordination. Thus we see that a counting error can fall into one of three categories each of which can be further subdivided, they are:

Point object error *Word and point coincide but does not point to correct object*
1. Double count.
2. Omit an item.
3. Starts not at 1st object.
4. Did not stop at end of array.
5. Stops before the end of array.
6. Points to objects in random order.

Word errors *Utterance of incorrect word*
7. Repeats a number.
8. Random numbers.
9. Reverses, 1, 2, 4, 3, 5.
10. Counts (N) but
11. Jumps back.
12. Jumps on.
13. Restarts at one.

Word point errors *Says correct word but points to the wrong object*
14. Several words to a point.
15. Several points to a word.
16. A word between points.
17. Points quicker than counts.
18. Says word but does not point.
19. Points but does not say count word.

Using a simple recording sheet, one can observe children's counting practices, recording which mistakes a child makes, and at what point along the counting string the mistakes are made. Gaining this knowledge helps one to assess which of the above rules a child has learnt and which have yet to be grasped.

For example:

A child has made *Point Object* errors and *Word* errors but no *Word point* errors. Most of these counting errors occurred within early numbers 0 to 5, above 5 the child made many word errors so was generally only given small sets of 4 or 5 to count. Thus one sees that the child can reliably say a counting word and make a pointing action at exactly the same time, but the child was often pointing to the wrong object, or pointing to an object twice etc. In an attempt to remedy this error I presented the child with many counting activities where she has to slowly pick up each object as she counts it. Most of these activities are presented within a fun activity or game.

Another child made a range of counting errors from all three categories, but mostly within higher numbers between 13 and 16. This shows that he had a good understanding of the first and second rules but probably did not know all the number words above 13. The third rule of cardinality can be taught and tested by activities as 'Give me' and 'How many?'. It is good to sometimes test children but most of one's maths teaching should be modelling as the child accompanies an adult correctly carrying out each activity. Cardinality is difficult for a child to grasp. Each counting word has both an ordinal and a cardinal meaning. As one counts four items, 'one, two, three, four', one is saying *ordinal* count words. When we have counted the last item we hold the number four in our head but from giving it an *ordinal* meaning one must now give it a *cardinal* meaning. This is a difficult task and a child will not conceptualise this skill until he is intellectually mature enough to grasp it. This does not mean that one should not present such a task to a child until he has demonstrated he is ready, as children will benefit from being exposed to activities even before mature enough to fully understand them.

A child who had grasped cardinality will shortly be working on the additional skill of counting on. This is an even more complicated concept and most children (mainstream as well as children with SLD) take a long time to grasp it. If a child is asked to add two numbers 3 and 2, and is given bricks to count with he will initially count three, 'one, two, three', given two more items he will count them beginning again at one, 'one, two, three, four, five'. In counting on the child needs to be able to move on from giving the three a *cardinal* meaning to give it an *ordinal* meaning, thus establishing not only that the first set contains three, but also to say 'three, four, five'. A technique used to teach this skill is to have two dice, one with numerals and one with dots. Using this equipment the child is compelled to count on from three and is not able to count the complete set again starting at one.

CONCLUSION

All of these teachers are describing work which involves a molecular approach, the breaking down of complex tasks into small components. Although this is more commonly attempted with children who have serious learning problems, the analysis of the processes of understanding in basic subjects enables the teacher to identify the nature of the difficulty, and to identify where the child is experiencing difficulty. Once this is understood, a teaching programme geared to the individual can begin.

Of course, teachers working with large classes will find such fine-tuned work difficult to organise. However, the sensitive use of SEN specialists and support teachers can provide the help which gets individual children over the hump, and the demonstration that this is possible helps more children to achieve.

8

Teachers and Whole-School Policies

Virtually every aspect of education has developed a 'language', a set of terms which allows its participants to converse around what appears, superficially at least, to be a shared continuum of concerns. Special education is no different. Teachers by and large seem to recognise certain commonly-held views when terms such as 'differentiation', 'pupils with problems', 'underachievement' and so on are under discussion. On a more general level, there has been widespread use of the expression 'whole-school policy', especially in the period after the 1981 Act (Dyson, Millward and Skidmore, 1994). There is often an accompanying expectation that such strategies are, without question, 'good', irrespective of the specific content of the policy.

The intimation that the whole-school approach in SEN is a panacea has been bred in part by the copious literature on the subject, which has lent respectability to the strategy. As a result it has often been the case that such policies have been written up and only given attention at particular periods in the school year – these tend frequently to coincide with OFSTED inspections. Bines (1993) has pointed out that, in a survey of whole-school policies (OFSTED, 1993), 'only half of the primary schools . . . had a written policy statement and not all of these had been fully implemented or evaluated. And although two-thirds of the secondary schools in the same survey had such policies, only half had put them into practice.'

The 1993 Education Act required that all schools must develop and publish an SEN policy. Advice relating to the formulation of such policies were enshrined in subsequent guidance from the DfE, which has tended to confirm the importance of adopting whole-school approaches when developing SEN policies. The primary focus of the Code of Practice (DfE, 1994) relates to work that teachers do in mainstream primary and secondary schools. In doing this it represents a significant shift in thinking from the guidance that accompanied the 1981 Act. Thus the requirements of the Code place the responsibility for meeting the SENs of pupils firmly in the context of the whole school. It explicitly states that 'While the governing body and the head teacher will take overall responsibility for the school's SEN policy, the school as a whole should be involved in its development' (para 2:10). Elsewhere it confirms that 'all teaching and non-teaching staff should be involved in the development of the

111

school's SEN policy' (para 2:7), whilst the practical outcomes of such an approach are given substance in the guidance that 'The child's class teacher or form/year tutor has overall responsibility' (para 2:72).

Such exhortations have to be viewed against the difficulty of ensuring that everyone is involved in decision-making. Whole-school policies have frequently come under criticism from the 'ordinary' teachers who have to implement them because they are seen as the products of deliberations by a small group of senior managers, their contents being viewed as directives. Such policies, whatever they may relate to, are treated with justifiable resentment by the workers who have not been invited to participate in their formulation. They exist on paper, and seem to be removed from the reality of classroom life (Palmer, Redfern & Smith, 1994). They are also indicative of a hierarchical approach to school organisation and management. 'Ownership', to coin a popular and politically correct term, is missing.

Moreover, as Bell, Stakes and Taylor (1994) have pointed out, the whole-school approach to SEN has caused particular difficulty in certain secondary schools where there is 'more didactic, teacher centred teaching with an emphasis on a class learning skills and there has been a greater tendency to group pupils by ability than in the primary schools'. Consequently, whilst Diniz (1991) emphasises the current trend of regarding every teacher as a teacher of special needs children, a view espoused by the Code of Practice, there are major difficulties involved in putting such a principle into practice.

The same, incidentally, can be said of those school policies which do not involve the children in their formulation and operation. Just like teachers, pupils can become alienated from the school's policies if they have not been allowed to participate in the decision-making which relates to them (Booth & Coulby, 1987). It is equally possible that they will also become cynical, detached and non-participative if they are only allowed to have a say in policy-making which does not threaten the status quo. The Code of Practice focuses mainly upon the identification and assessment of special needs. Its recommendation to schools that they should involve pupils in decision-making processes needs to be given wider currency, so that it covers more general whole-school matters, including policies relating to discipline, curriculum, school organisation and so on. Pupils are the bedrock for determining 'ethos', and it is our view that this should develop *from them*, rather than given *to them*, as 'helpings' of what is good for them. The resultant sense of 'belonging' felt by pupils is an important determinant of a positive ethos (Mongon & Hart, 1989). Once again, the parallels with teachers themselves are very powerful.

Each of the three themes outlined above (the overall coherence, relevance and enabling features of a whole-school policy, the involvement of teachers and of pupils in their formulation) establish the *principles* on which the whole-school policy is based. In the extracts of teachers' work contained in this chapter a record is provided of their struggle to give some definition to the philosophy which, they believe, ought to underpin formal or informal whole-school policies, relating not only to SEN as a whole but to related aspects of school activity, notably the behaviour of children. Whilst there is no suggestion here that children who have SEN will automatically display unacceptable or anti-social behaviour in school, it is nevertheless the case that whole-school behaviour policies have been seen by many teachers as synonymous with one discrete aspect of SEN, the school's approach to children who are deemed to have emotional and/or behavioural difficulties (EBD). What all of these observations suggest is that little can be taken for granted when either formulating or putting into practice a set of guiding principles which define whole-school policies relating to SEN.

But it is equally important to consider the actual *content* of the SEN policy: this is sometimes overlooked, with little time being allocated to discussion on what should comprise a school's overall approach to SEN. Palmer et al. (1994) identified seven elements of a whole-school SEN policy: factual information, school responsibilities, equal opportunities, curriculum, identification, assessment and intervention, parents as partners and collaboration. These coincide with the current framework for school inspection used by OFSTED.

In order to assess the *effectiveness* of their SEN policies schools are advised in the Code to report on the systems they put in place for identification, assessment, provision, monitoring/record keeping and the use of outside agencies (para 2:12). It is therefore worth while considering the extent to which each of these aspects of policy are viewed as being representative of a 'shared' endeavour by teachers, who are the focal point of SEN intervention, especially as an ability to demonstrate effective school-wide systems for implementation and monitoring of policy will 'be an important element of inspection and may help to offset concern about a particular area of policy which has not yet been fully addressed in practice' (Bines, 1993).

The three strands to be borne in mind when considering the observations that teachers make about whole-school policy therefore cover both implementation of policy and the substance of what is introduced, as well as some means by which the policy can be evaluated. The first two are integral to the successful operation of a whole-school approach, as measured by the opportunities it provides to assist the development of children's academic and social learning. Each of these elements should then be subsumed in a policy plan, in which an ethos of shared activity is fostered and where 'individuals and groups within the school each have an opportunity to set the agenda and express views' (Bines, 1993) so that the necessary framework is put in place so that 'children may use as of right the general facilities available at school and also receive the special help that they require' (DES, 1978).

Many of the teachers contributing to this book comment positively about the way they see their role in whole-school curriculum planning and provision for children who have SEN. Indicative of a general belief that discussion and collaboration form the essential bedrock for successful intervention is one primary-school teacher's observation that:

Ideally I would like to see a whole school approach to the problem [of identification and assessment to ensure an appropriately differentiated curriculum]. Firstly those with curriculum expertise would lay down guidelines and ensure that everything was covered correctly with no omissions or repetitions. Secondly the whole school should be involved in building up a bank of resources and materials which are stored in an easily accessible way. These could be updated or manipulated if required. Thirdly there should be careful planning for the use of support staff. This is the ideal. At the moment I feel that my institution is limping somewhat hesitantly towards it. There is a lot more planning going on although there needs to be more liaison between the various phases. More materials and resources are being purchased or made for a central store, but at the moment teachers seem reluctant to donate their worksheets to this store. There seems to be very little evaluation of the work provided or how the lesson went. (L. G.)

In the above passage, L. G. is effectively summarising some of the most important elements of whole-school policies. But the extract is also indicative of the inherent dangers in the assumption that simply by having a policy, children with learning difficulties will be protected. As Lewis (1991, p. 6) has observed, there is a danger that 'whole school policies on learning difficulties may be only a facade, masking rather than confronting the issues by recording on paper policies and statements of principles but not translating them into practice'. L. G. acknowledges this by referring to the hesitant limp towards a policy for the use of support staff. She notices 'more planning' taking place but some of the practicalities of translating this into actions which will affect children in classrooms (for example, in some teachers' reluctance to share curriculum materials) clearly weigh heavily on her mind.

Another teacher (W. S.), working in a special school, provides an example of a formal strategy adopted by his school to assist in the process of reviewing a given area of the curriculum (see p. 115).

This is a crucial element in enabling children with learning difficulties to have access to a wide set of experiences and as such represents an essential area for whole-school development. It is therefore not surprising that some authors (for example, Lewis (1991) link curriculum development and whole-school approaches inextricably together.

This example serves to show the importance which teachers assign to collaboration, and for the establishment of a set of shared goals, themselves hallmarks of successful whole-school policies. It is noticeable that this strategy contains phrases such as 'all members are involved', 'responsibilities shared', 'team relationships', and so on. It is, moreover, not by accident that the notion of 'team membership' is firmly embedded in the overall strategy. Such cooperation, and the planning of curriculum interventions by negotiation between all concerned, is central to what is now popularly known as 'effective teaching' (Ainscow, 1990).

In the previous chapter, Z. R. described a detailed programme of number teaching. He commented that the programme, carried out in a collaborative

Criteria	Scale	Comments
Management structure - a clear structure is in place and all members are involved - responsibilities are shared within the team KS3/KS4/GCSE/CoE/IT/reading/library/ purchasing materials etc) - team members' expertise and interests utilized effectively		
Communications - coordinator listens and provides direction - regular meetings - agenda circulated in advance - minutes circulated to team and SMT - team involved in decision making - regular links with other curriculum areas		
Job descriptions - role of coordinator documented - specific roles for other team members		
Staffing - staffing matches needs of the curriculum - adequate expertise within the teaching team - adequate expertise within support staff - support staff utilized effectively - support staff have a clearly defined role within the classroom which is commonly understood		
Team work - team relationships good - all members feel valued		
Curriculum development plan - long and short term planning is documented - targets set are achievable - the process of staff involvement in curriculum development planning is understood		

organisation, had implications beyond the participants, and helped to extend whole-school awareness:

It was enjoyable working with a different group of children; to be able to visit and work with another colleague's classroom broadens one's experience. I felt that perhaps this was a way forward towards sharing our expertise and areas of interest; visiting or working in each others' rooms diminishes the possibility of staff feeling isolated or unsupported. Problems with implementing the curriculum or assessing children's needs can be discussed and shared. The experience has also provided me with some ideas to bring into the teaching programme with my own class. The experience of assessing children's needs and then setting precise short term targets was a valuable one. A recent INSET day in school focused on planning for short term targets, this experience relates very well to these goals.

Although not a great deal of 'new' material emerged from the project, perhaps some of the worksheets/record sheets may be useful for future maths work across the school. The Mathsteps programme is available to each teacher, this bank of activities can be a useful basic structure for planning and doing mathematical activities with the children. Perhaps I was able to show in a small way how maths can be drawn out at or related to other curriculum areas such as music or creative work. (Z. R.)

It is apparent that there is a high degree of awareness amongst teachers that a school policy, even where it has been developed in a cooperative way, has to be seen to be effective in a practical sense. In other words it needs to have an impact on what and how children learn. A series of observations by B. A., who teaches in a special school for children who have MLD and/or EBD, illustrates the tension which teachers see between the rhetoric of 'paper policy' and the reality of its implementation:

As a school we have tried to provide some continuity in how children learn. Each day begins with one hour of Basic Skills. During this lesson children are given an explanation of what they are being asked to complete in reading, writing/handwriting and number and then the teacher helps individual children while the classroom assistant listens to readers or vice-versa. This is a very formal lesson where children are expected to work alone in their seats, asking for help when necessary. The second lesson tends to be Maths-related and then the third and fourth lessons are dedicated to the remainder of the curriculum. Apart from the first lesson of the day, teaching and learning styles range from the didactic to collaborative. Most of the staff tend to use one teaching style most of the time. This created some noticeable problems at the beginning of a new term as children go into new classes. For children who have followed a fairly didactic learning style the previous year, to enter a class where a more independent learning approach is used and the children are encouraged to contribute to classroom organization, planning etc., is sometimes too much for some children to handle initially. These children find the boundaries have been moved out too quickly and the teacher must then quickly adjust. In the same way, to suddenly have restrictions placed on one's actions has caused some children to react against the restricted boundaries. We have seen that a variety of teaching and learning styles need to be used in each class so that children can maintain some continuity in learning as they progress through the school. Already this term we have begun to discuss as a staff what is a 'successful' classroom and a policy on teaching and learning styles has been drafted.

In the preceding passage it is clear that a number of principles which govern whole-school approaches to SEN provision are seen as critical areas in which teachers have to make collective decisions. What B. A. is pointing out is that for teaching and learning to be effective the child who has SEN must be presented with a coherent and intelligible range of experiences. As B. A. also suggests, schools require a negotiated policy to ensure that contradictions do not occur, not least in the mind of the child, who may be unable to decode the messages hidden in the variety of teaching styles adopted by the staff and therefore become confused. But this uniformity may negate many potential developments in classrooms. Instead of providing a means of enabling teachers and learners to function more effectively, they become strait-jackets which inhibit innovation and flair from individuals. Many of the authors in this section present evidence of their struggle, and that of their colleagues, to come to terms with the dilemmas thus posed.

Similar concerns underpin the assessment of pupils who have SEN. Without a shared understanding of the purpose of assessment, together with a recognition that such approaches must be accessible to all staff, the value of what follows – the curriculum intervention – will be eroded. The Code of Practice calls for uniformity, stating that the initial stage will reveal 'the different perceptions of those concerned with the child' (para 2:76). The Code recommends that discussion should follow, in which the class teacher and the SEN coordinator will arrive at a decision as to the best course of action. There is a presumption that the protocols and format of a whole-school SEN policy will be followed in this process. The need for schools to adopt such an approach has been recognised by SEAC (1990), who emphasised the links between teaching, learning and assessment. Notwithstanding this official recognition, however, there remains a great deal of confusion, as one of our contributors notes:

At the moment there are so many different ways of assessing pupils that the usefulness of these assessments isn't always immediately apparent. As the school's methods of assessing pupils' progress evolves then staff may use this information from previous years in their current planning. However, until we decide as a staff, first of all, how we will assess pupils and, second, what we want these assessments to tell us, they will be of little use. (B. A.)

Nevertheless, the difficulties that schools have in securing a shared policy which will 'affect practice, and meet the real needs of children, parents and staff' (Gross, 1993) are commonplace. Teachers in both mainstream and special schools face numerous problems in arriving at uniform approaches to each stage of policy formulation (principles, content and evaluation). Secondary schools face particular difficulties in establishing uniform approaches, given their organisation into discrete subject departments or areas, and a parallel structure for pastoral care. Even within those 'faculties' which link related subject-specialisms together there can be acute problems stemming from a tradition of individual and separate teaching and, to an extent, an implicit rivalry between subject specialists. Illustrating this point, E. J. writes that 'None of the three [humanities] subject areas has a stated or written policy on differentiation and there is no collaborative planning or preparation for this at present.'

In matters of general organisation, several of our contributors notice that their schools function in ways which are not conducive to the involvement of all staff in policy formulation. This, it should be stated, is a theme which surfaces at several points in recent official documents concerning SEN (notably the Code of Practice and the 'Pupils with Problems' circulars). It is noticeable that even relatively small primary and special schools can be prone to the detrimental effects of 'top-down', exclusive management styles. The reader gathers a genuine sense of resignation (and possibly withdrawal) in L. G.'s remark that 'The school has a hierarchy of management. The senior management team has regular weekly meetings to discuss the general running of the school and school policy.'

B. A. is more directly critical of this style of school management:

The Senior Management Team in our school consists of Headteacher, Deputy Headteacher and Senior Teacher, who is class based. Despite efforts by the Headteacher to 'empower' all staff I have found through observation and personal experience that some decisions made by staff when empowered have been vetoed by the Headteacher.

In spite of these cautionary tales, however, there is an overall sense of common purpose in the accounts that teachers give of their work in school. This is encouraging, given that the concept of a 'whole-school' approach in education in general, let alone in SEN, is as yet a relatively new one, having been adapted by teachers from the principle of 'language *across the curriculum*', first used in the Bullock Report (DES, 1975). Roaf (1989) notes that the first article to examine the term 'whole-school policy' in relation to SEN was as late as 1985. So things have come a long way, and most teachers now recognise that whole-school approaches are essential.

L. G., for example, reports on the gathering pace of developments in her school and on the widespread acceptance amongst her colleagues for common approaches in both learning and social behaviours:

Last year a draft behaviour policy was written for the school. Some members of the staff had been on courses dealing with behaviour and their knowledge and experience was drawn on by the working party. It was agreed that 'A whole-school approach to learning and behaviour difficulties is increasingly seen as synonymous with meeting children's special needs'. (Wolfendale, 1987)

On a more personal level, another primary-school teacher reflects upon her belief-systems which, whilst clearly implying its importance on the way in which she might teach, shows also that the personal philosophy she has adopted has important ramifications for policy developments in her school:

I believe in sharing my thinking and perceptions. I acknowledge the difficulties in this process particularly when opposition to change/ideas abounds. But I believe that imposition demotivates the profession and involvement in the process is the key element. (N. B.)

Whole-school policies have been used in the past to address such curriculum issues as handwriting, marking of children's work and information technology. In fact, it is interesting to note that the emphasis given to 'cross curricular themes' in the National Curriculum, a process for which collective responsibility is assumed by the whole staff, represents a natural extension of this school-wide involvement. For many teachers involved in SEN, this way of working has become commonplace, with one teacher noting, almost in a matter of fact manner, that 'A "Whole Curriculum approach" which will assist in finding ways to adapt the curriculum so that all children (including those with SEN) can participate in and derive benefit from all areas of learning is the way forward' (L. C.).

Earlier in this chapter we noted that whole-school policies have been traditionally used to cover aspects of schooling which, whilst not expressly devoted to SEN, are nevertheless closely related to children's progress in both formal and informal school activities. Once more there is evidence that most schools have at least begun to wrestle with the problems of devising and implementing such holistic strategies. A typical example of this is the dilemma surrounding children for whom English is not the first language; difficulties relating to assessment, coupled with the sometimes inappropriate behaviour of some of these children resulting from sheer frustration at not being able to maintain a mother-tongue approach to learning, has resulted in many being categorised as having an SEN. The reporting of one teacher indicates again the level of importance given to a uniform, consistent approach across the whole institution. Thus, the teacher deduced that:

Integration must therefore imply mutual support and collaboration between language teachers and subject teachers for the educational benefit of pupils, and that collaboration implies a search for a common agenda. This also implicitly demands cooperation in the planning stage . . . But unless a whole-school policy is in place at the planning and organising stages the teaching styles for differentiation cannot operate. (L. C.)

For many teachers it is in a school's adoption of a whole-school policy to discipline and behaviour that the benefits of such approaches are best summarised. As we have indicated, there are important overlaps between social and cognitive behaviours to consider when assessing a child's learning difficulty. Often, unacceptable behaviour is a product of a pupil's inability to grasp certain academic skills and concepts. It follows that the way in which a whole-school policy on behaviour is developed and operationalised will have great significance to the SEN child, his teachers and others contributing to the educational process.

Circular 8/94, entitled 'Pupil Behaviour and Discipline' (DfE, 1994), tacitly reaffirms the official view that pupils should be involved in the development of schools' behaviour policies. In stating that 'They should be worked out cooperatively' (p. 3) the circular is reinforcing the advice promoted by the Elton Report (1989) that the views of pupils should be taken into account in matters relating to school discipline.

Both documents (the Elton Report and Circular 8/94), together with the Code of Practice, stop somewhere short of directly recommending that pupils should, as a matter of course, be involved in helping to make decisions about school policy. Nevertheless there can be little doubt that these publications do represent a step forward, in seeing children who have special needs not as 'fixed', uni-dimensional individuals but as active agents in their own school lives. This is recognised by many of the teachers whose work is represented in this book.

L. G., for example, recognises the value of cooperative decision-making in this area, believing that it helps to maximise the resources and expertise of the whole staff. She argues, for instance, that

Many of the staff attend courses on dealing with behaviour problems, working with outside agencies and helping children with special needs in class, but little time is given for them to report back to the rest of their colleagues and perhaps introduce some new ideas into the school. I would like to see this done on a much more formal basis with ideas being discussed among the staff and then studies being carried out and monitored.

In moving towards a policy which reflected a consensus in the school, a series of incremental steps were taken. L. G. goes on to provide a narrative of this process:

The school has made a start in the right direction by introducing a behaviour policy and structuring the management of the school to give staff as much support as possible. Policies are continually being looked at and updated.

The aim of the school's policy was stated as follows – to enable all children to develop a sense of self discipline, together with respect for others and their environment. The working group accepted the premise that 'It is acknowledged that buildings, space, room layout (visible features) as well as personnel deployment, interaction between personnel, hierarchies, communication links, organisation (less immediately visible features) are profoundly influential upon the efficient working of any institution or organisation' (Wolfendale, 1987). Consequently it concentrated on particular areas including entering school, lunchtimes and playground behaviour. It was felt that if the children came into school in an orderly manner and if they were not always getting into trouble at break and lunchtimes they would be in a more receptive mood for learning. (L. G.)

It may be argued that this kind of policy development largely excludes the wishes of children and parents. It is also very much a top-down process of development, a weakness which L. G. herself acknowledges, stating that 'there are many weaknesses . . . There is still the feeling that the problem should be shifted onto someone else's shoulders – the teacher has enough to cope with, dealing with thirty odd children in the class', and that 'The staff are not together in ensuring that the rules are always adhered to'.

But the gradual change of attitude has been occurring as schools come under increasing scrutiny through more regular inspection. There are indications that teachers are becoming aware that the ways in which pupil-opinion is sought, assimilated and acted upon will become an important indicator of school-effectiveness. This is signalled, for example, in Framework 4 of the current school inspection manual, which uses the question 'Do the school's arrangements encourage all pupils to contribute to school life and to exercise responsibility?' (OFSTED, 1993). Immediately, then, both principle and pragmatism form the rationale for measures designed to incorporate the views of pupils in helping to develop policies.

Consequently, there has been more proactive use made of various ways of obtaining the views of pupils, as one teacher from a special school has indicated:

In the drawing up of a whole school policy on behaviour we are going through various processes. Our first was to consult with the young people themselves by way of the School Council to identify actions which they feel constitute bad behaviour and indeed how they felt it should be dealt with. (P. Q.)

CONCLUSION

The commentaries included in this chapter present more reason for anticipation and hopefulness than for despair. They are indicative of the efforts of classroom and other teachers to meet ever-increasing demands on their time and expertise at a time of unprecedented change in compulsory education. It is true there are occasions when a sense of frustration may give rise to a more narrow, teacher-centred viewpoint. But the evidence for this is relatively thin on the ground. Ultimately, therefore, teachers have demonstrated a willingness to assume a collective responsibility for SEN, and to share in decision-making with other professionals, children and parents. The progress made is accurately summed up by a primary SEN coordinator, who comments that

Curriculum planning has been the responsibility of the classroom teacher and individual programmes the responsibility of the Special Needs Coordinator. On reflection it may be valuable to work together in this process . . . if a class teacher has not been involved in the design of the individual programme then they often forget about its existence and it becomes ineffective. (V. Q.)

SECTION 4
Teachers and Behaviour

Introduction

There can be little doubt that one of the prime concerns of anyone involved in education is the way in which children's unacceptable behaviour is managed. As most teachers know, everyone likes to have their say where topics such as 'disruptive pupils', 'problem behaviour or discipline' are concerned. 'Behaviour', to many, is synonymous with 'bad behaviour'.

This 'behaviour' has become a recurrent theme in education in the twentieth century during which concerns about declining standards have been repeatedly highlighted (Frude and Gault, 1984). That these concerns are indicative more of a moral panic rather than of any real increase in the levels of unacceptable behaviour in schools is nicely summarised by Everhart (1983), who has commented that 'Media exposure to such issues as physical attacks on teachers and the use of drugs in school might suggest that most public concern about school discipline amounts to concern about these sensationalized incidents', a view supported by HMI (DES, 1989b).

Whatever the truth of the matter, there can be little doubt that there has for a long time been considerable pressure on teachers to 'do something' about the (perceived) problem. It is therefore unsurprising that, in recent years, various official reports have each recommended certain courses of action by teachers which are useful in maintaining 'good discipline'.

But why should these concerns form part of a volume devoted to SEN? Are we not reinforcing the belief that unacceptable behaviour in school automatically becomes the concern of the SEN teachers, and the first indications of emotional and or behavioural difficulty? We would argue a case from two perspectives.

Firstly, children's ability to participate in, and benefit from, the taught curriculum is seriously impaired when their behaviour in the classroom is such that it is disruptive both to the child engaging in the behaviour and to those around him. There has, consequently, long been an acceptance that inappropriate behaviour and underachievement go hand in hand. The teacher who works closely with issues surrounding underachievement cannot help but be involved in resolving inappropriate behaviour.

But there are other behaviours which cause concern which are indicative of more deep seated emotional problems. These have become the almost exclusive property of special schools and involve the difficulties presented by children who have been assessed as having EBD, children who have autistic tendencies, or who are identified as having severe learning difficulties and who display 'challenging behaviour'.

It is the latter term which we have decided to use as descriptive of the collective behaviours described above. In doing so we recognise that, like the expression 'disruptive pupil', the term will mean different things to different people. What follows therefore are accounts of teachers who work in a variety of contexts with children whose behaviour, in that context, is seen as challenging.

9

Teachers and Challenging Behaviour

Behaviour of which we disapprove or which we find threatening or disturbing has carried a range of descriptors. Gradually we have abandoned words like 'delinquent', 'maladjusted', 'disruptive', 'disturbed', as each assumed a pejorative connotation. The current phrase 'emotional and behavioural difficulties' has already become problematic. In an attempt to separate the act from the actor, and thus allow the behaviour to be disapproved of without denigrating the behaver, a new convention has arisen: 'challenging' behaviour. This echoes the political correctness which describes the blind (often to their disgust) as 'visually challenged' but it does have the advantage that the behaviour can be seen to be a challenge to the individual who behaves in certain unacceptable ways, as well as to the observer, or recipient. It also allows us to concentrate on the behaviour as an interpersonal act, in which the antecedents and consequences of the behaviour which initiate or maintain it may be seen as originating with the observer as much as with the behaver. Thus the behaviour can be seen to have extrinsic as well as intrinsic roots, which in turn helps us to understand and, hopefully, to change it.

A convention has developed in recent years whereby 'challenging behaviour' is used solely to describe the behaviour of children with severe learning difficulties. In our view this is unfortunate, for any of the above definitions could be used to describe behaviour which teachers in other settings, including mainstream schools, find 'challenging'. The very fact that such behaviour is situation-specific and that different teachers have different views about what it constitutes, means that studying the ways of working in one sector may be rewarding for those who work in other kinds of institution.

A CHALLENGE TO THE SYSTEM

In chapter 3, we saw how, in an educational context, approaches which concentrate on the actual learning behaviour of children (including behavioural approaches and task analysis) have proved to be highly effective aids in teaching new skills to children with SEN, including those with the most severe learning difficulties. Essentially the same techniques have been used by professionals in some residential contexts to replace, change and control the behaviour of people with learning difficulties who present severe challenging behaviour. Historically, those who presented the most severely challenging behaviour lived away from the community in severe subnormality hospitals. Post 1970 the younger residents lived and were educated in the same institution, attending hospital schools during the day and sleeping on the wards at night. The quality of life for residents and staff in these institutions was often poor, the buildings were unsuitable, staff turnover was high and morale was low. It was obvious to most that it was the environment which maintained the maladaptive behaviours; it was the environment which needed changing, not the residents' behaviour. However, working in difficult conditions, staff in such institutions were in a Catch 22 situation; they may have seen some justification in the way residents presented challenging behaviour as a means of objecting to their situation; but they were powerless to offer any real alternatives, the large institutions were these people's homes for life. So nurses, psychologists and psychiatrists looked towards medication and behavioural approaches to modify the residents' more severe challenging behaviour and to resign them to their fate. Drugs and aversive forms of behaviour management at least offered some hope of maintaining the status quo.

Some of the management techniques used in these institutions to modify people's behaviour were particularly unpleasant. In the United States these methods included severe aversive stimuli, even including electric shock. Britain never went quite so far down the strong aversives route as North America; however, 'time-out' rooms were sometimes used more as solitary confinement rather than as temporary respite, and splints and harnesses for some became the norm. Unlike in some states in the USA and Canada, where the cattle-prod was shown to be successful in modifying behaviour, contingent electric shock was rarely used in Britain and only in circumstances when challenging behaviour became life-threatening, e.g., when continued self-injurious behaviour (e.g., head-banging) would have resulted in death.

Most of these old hospitals have now been closed or pulled down. The principle of normalisation has encouraged care in the community. For some of the mentally ill, care in the community has meant a sleeping bag or a cardboard box in a shop window. For many people with learning difficulties, it has meant only close proximity to the community; minimal real integration has taken place. For those people who presented severe challenging behaviour, even this proximity was short-lived. They soon found themselves in a secure wing, albeit in a community hospital. At least in a severe subnormality hospital they did not have unrealistic demands placed upon them, and some could roam free in the grounds.

The circumstances awaiting children in the mainstream whose behaviour gives cause for concern may not be so extreme. It is, however, the case that teachers, in seeking to help children to cope with their experiences in school, do so not only for short-term managerial reasons, or to allow other children to work effectively, but also in order to help prevent that adult maladjustment which may otherwise await these same children in later years. (So, are the lives of people who present severe challenging behaviour any better? In terms of schooling, we would say definitely, yes.) The extracts which follow are written by teachers with a strong commitment to protecting the interests of young people with learning difficulties who present challenging behaviour. Recent legislation and higher standards of professional practice have meant that some of the stronger aversive practices referred to earlier are no longer tolerated in schools. The Children Act has encouraged professionals to focus on ethical issues and has helped to ensure that individual staff members' responses to children's severe challenging behaviour are chosen with reference to what is in the paramount interests of the individual child (Section 1i Children Act 1989). However, the legal issues relating to the Children Act are still subject to considerable interpretation as there is no specific mention in the Act of children with learning difficulties who also present challenging behaviour. We now live in a climate of greater concern about human rights; and the advocacy movement has done much to protect the rights of people with learning disability (Garner and Sandow, 1995).

The teaching profession is also more committed to the notion of reflective practice; more than ever before teachers seek to refine their teaching by evaluating their work, drawing on theory to inform their practice and looking critically at the way in which their values and expectations affect their teaching. This is combined with a new determination to respect the child as a participant in the education process, rather than a simple recipient. These two factors underpin the work of those concerned with severe challenging behaviour, as well as those coping with disruption in ordinary schools.

WHAT IS CHALLENGING BEHAVIOUR?

Challenging behaviour has been defined by Emerson et al. (1987) as behaviour which prevents children's 'participation in appropriate educational activities; isolates them from their peers; affects the learning and functioning of other pupils; drastically reduces their opportunities for involvement in ordinary community activities; makes excessive demands on teachers, staff and resources; places the child or others in physical danger; and makes the possibilities for future placement difficult'.

Emerson (op. cit.) goes on to say that severe challenging behaviour 'is not a transient phenomenon', that is, people who present a challenge to a service, whatever service they find themselves in, will do so for a considerable period of time. The Mental Health Foundation (Lyon, 1944) states that, as such behaviour represents a challenge to services, definitions are 'therefore based on social judgements (what challenges one service or institution may not challenge another) and definitions must be considered in context' (p. 4). F. F. writes about such social judgements, but in reference to individual staff members:

N. displays a number of challenging behaviours, the most obvious of which involve some type of physical attack. Although not a large or apparently strong person, her strength can multiply enormously when she 'locks' into the person she is attacking . . . For some time now there has been a generally held view that N. 'targets' certain members of staff. While this is true in part, unfortunately some staff have allowed this to deteriorate into a personal antagonism between them and N. Due to staff concern about this issue, and their belief that negative feedback magnifies N.'s behaviour, strategies for positive interaction have been written into her policy. Indeed the negative agendas that are found around N. support the claim of Jones and Miller (1994) that it is the challenge of the behaviour to the service that needs reflection and adaptation rather than the behaviour itself. They rightly interpret challenging behaviour as a 'complex matrix of interactions' some of which are socially constructed. While not invalidating .the distress experienced while encountering one of N.'s attacks, it is clear that negative attitudes only fuel her behaviour.

J. K. talks about 'personal, cultural and theoretical bias and prejudices playing a direct role in interpretation of challenging behaviour', and S. G. states that the nature of challenging behaviour, its definitions and implications can perhaps quite clearly be seen as subjective and ambiguous. S. G. states:

definitions may be hard to come by when individuals' perceptions on what is and what is not challenging are naturally so diverse and personalised . . . and one's perceptions of what is and what is not challenging largely depends upon the resources and expertise available at the time. (Jones and Miller, 1994)

S. G. adds:

the behaviours which are considered challenging depend upon individual staff members' individual levels of tolerance and these are affected by their values and prejudices, together with the stresses they are experiencing at a particular time.

Although these extracts come from the work of teachers in SLD schools, it is clear that any one of them could apply to teaching and learning in other settings. Children in ordinary schools have been observed to 'target' certain teachers while behaving quite acceptably with others. Management by negative feedback, such as punishment without concomitant reward for good behaviour, sarcasm, 'pre-emptive strikes', or group punishment often feature in teachers' agendas, and often help to maintain the behaviour instead of eliminating it. It is a commonplace that schools in different areas have different levels of tolerance, and what is acceptable behaviour in one place may be anathema in another. Even within one school, different teachers have different ideas of what is appropriate, and 'he's perfectly all right with me' is a less than helpful way of achieving consensus.

WAYS OF LOOKING AT BEHAVIOUR

The Gentle Teaching movement in the early 1980s did much to focus people's attention away from seeing challenging behaviour as a 'within child' phenomenon. McGee and colleagues looked at staff response to challenging behaviour. McGee advocated a non-aversive, 'gentle' approach to behaviour management, with an emphasis on the 'posture and attitude' of the care-giver and on 'human engagement' (Menolascino and McGee, 1983; McGee et al., 1987). Gentle Teaching aimed to develop 'bonding interdependence through gentleness, respect and solidarity' (Jones and Connell, 1993). Central to its philosophy was an 'unconditional valuing' of the person, irrespective of his or her behaviour (McGee et al., 1987) and a commitment to 'mutual change', where care-givers analyse and increase their 'value-centred interactions and decrease dominative ones'.

The effectiveness of Gentle Teaching as an intervention strategy is difficult to evaluate. However, the Gentle Teaching movement did raise humanitarian questions about aversive approaches and its focus on holistic education directed attention to the values and expectations of the people who work with people who have challenging behaviour.

Nind and Hewett's (1994) 'intensive interaction' has clearly been influenced by the Gentle Teaching movement. H. H. and her staff are strongly committed to assuming a more approachable and tolerant posture:

We try to look at the world through the eyes of the pupils and are often not surprised at all at some of the challenging behaviour. R. is a lively and energetic person – I'm not surprised that she runs into other classes. They probably look quite interesting. Being confined in a limited space for several hours a day, she is quite naturally going to run or dance down the corridor, or make a dash for an open space. By accepting these responses and understanding them, one's attitude changes and the element of negativeness recedes . . . Domination of another person, a highly used technique, is ultimately not successful, because as soon as the dominating person is not there to dominate, control is lost. Anyway, what are we trying to gain by being this way?

Looking at behaviour from the point of view of the 'behaver' is also appropriate whatever the level or degree of the aberrant behaviour, as shall be seen.

THE FUNCTIONS OF CHALLENGING BEHAVIOUR

Functional analysis of people's challenging behaviour offers greater insight into the reasons why they present such behaviour. The work of Iwatta et al. (1990), Durand and Carr (1990), Murphy (1985) and Zarowska and Clements (1988) indicated that, just as disruptive behaviour serves a purpose for the disrupter, challenging behaviour even on the part of the individual with PMLD can serve a recognisable purpose for the individual. Functional analysis derived from systematic observation of the child's behaviour in specific contexts can lead to testable hypotheses about setting events, e.g., an individual may engage in self-injurious behaviour to escape from unpleasant situations or demands. A person may engage in stereotypic routines for self-stimulation, may become aggressive to obtain tangible rewards, e.g., food, or may present violent behaviour for attention seeking reasons. Functional analysis can throw up a series of research questions. Functional analysis of the possible reasons for challenging behaviour in specific contexts can indicate testable hypotheses for future intervention. For example, how can the antecedents or consequences of children's behaviour be manipulated to reduce the likelihood of similar behaviour in similar situations? Can the child who regularly involves herself in stereotypic behaviours, e.g., hair-pulling, be encouraged to engage in an activity which is incompatible with hair-pulling, e.g., playing with a wind-up toy? Can the aggressive child be taught more acceptable ways of asking for an edible? We know that the functions of challenging behaviour and the functions of communication may be related (Carr and Durand, 1985). If the individual cannot reliably affect the behaviours of others using words or signs, or if his or her attempts to communicate are not responded to, then it is possible that alternative, less desirable, but equally effective means of communication such as aggression may be adopted instead. Moreover, it is likely that just such acts of aggression will be responded to, and therefore it can become learned behaviour.

J. P. summarises the possible functions of challenging behaviour (adapted from Durand, 1990):

Social attention
It is possible that an individual's challenging behaviour may be used as a tool for attracting the attention of others, e.g., a child who presents self-injurious behaviour may be using it as a strategy for gaining the attention of an individual, such as the class teacher or the school nurse. The resulting attention (although necessary in most cases) may therefore actually be maintaining the self-injurious behaviour.

Tangible consequences
Challenging behaviour may be presented by an individual in order that he or she can achieve a tangible reward, e.g., food or a favoured toy, or to prevent the removal of such a reward.

Sensory feedback
The sensory consequences of certain behaviours may serve to maintain them. For example, the child who headbangs may enjoy the sensation of flashing lights in front of his or her eyes, or the child who pulls hair may find the tactile feel from the hair pleasurable.

Escape
The child may be using challenging behaviour to opt out of a situation that he

or she finds aversive, e.g., an activity that contains unrealistic or unpleasant demands.

Multiple influences
Individuals may present challenging behaviour to serve different functions in different situations, or different functions in the same situations, e.g., the child may headbang on one occasion to avoid an aversive situation, or on another to get social attention.

OBSERVATION

S. G. formulates a series of questions which may relate to the function of a child's behaviour and which will form the focus for systematic observation:

- What is the nature of the task?
- Who is working with the child and what is the pupil staff ratio?
- How long does the activity last?
- Are the task demands and expectations reasonable?
- If the child presents challenging behaviour, what is it, how is it shown, what is the duration/frequency/intensity, what are the antecedents and consequences and what purpose does it serve for the child?

In the mainstream classroom, detailed and systematic observation is just as appropriate. K. P. writes:

Written comments . . . reveal that he was a 'loner and could be spiteful to other children'. As he progressed through the middle school a downward spiral can be observed and by the end of Year 11 both class teacher and headteacher were concerned enough to invite the mother into school and suggest psychological assessment . . . Looking through his record card it would seem that his teachers in the first school were satisfied with his progress. Discussion with the headteacher revealed that she was very concerned about the child for the following reasons:
- academically he was underachieving badly
- she could not seem to 'get through' to him on any level when trying to reason with him
- he seemed to be unemotional about most things
- he said he did not care about the effects of his actions on himself
- or others
- he had a poor self image.
The class teacher revealed an even longer list of problems, including:
- lack of care and concentration in his work
- very poor self image
- can be violent
- disruptive in class – attention seeking
- has a lethargic attitude

- is not liked by other children.

I used checklists and further questioning in an attempt to define the problems more specifically, asking 'but what does he actually do when he is being disruptive/lethargic/attention seeking'. The class teacher said that this was really useful and it helped her to think about what was actually going on and clarify events. Finally she decided that the behaviours which caused most annoyance and disruption were:

- calling out
- making noises
- challenging teacher's instructions.

We established the priorities for change:
the child would try to speak at appropriate times only
be more cooperative by following teacher's instructions.

I visited the classroom several times to observe the child in different situations. In art and science he was quietly getting on with his (practical) work and in drama he cooperated, listened to others and remained on task. Teachers were moving around the room encouraging and helping. I noticed that it was with the class teacher in a language lesson that he was most noticeable. He did call out and make noises and after each interruption looked round at the rest of the class. He was well rewarded. Each time the class teacher stopped mid-flow to remonstrate with him, other children sniggered.

MANAGING THE PROBLEM, INVOLVING THE STUDENT

Following this initial observation, the support teacher discussed with the boy M. the reasons for his misbehaviour. He clearly understood this, and agreed that calling out was his worst problem: 'It's always getting me into trouble . . . I do it when I get impatient if I can't write fast enough or make silly spelling mistakes . . . I just shout'. The next day M. agreed to monitor his own 'calling outs' between 9.00 am and 12 am. The teacher also kept her own tally, and at the end of the morning they agreed he had called out eight times:

We discussed the calling out and some strategies which M. could use when he felt unable to write fast enough. These included:
- ask class or support teacher for help (or teacher to be aware and offer help before the crisis)
- sit next to helpful pupil
- don't worry too much about spelling, this can be corrected later.

A 'contract' was set up between the child and the teacher, which included quiet praise, extra time to finish science or art and also a weekly report to his mother. However, the next stage demonstrated that contracts are bilateral agreements: both sides must keep the bargain:

I returned to school some ten days later – unsolicited feedback came immediately from another member of staff (not the class teacher). The boy had been noticable for his *good* behaviour! I spoke to the Deputy Head – another good report – no calling out had been noticed. I spoke to the class teacher – she reported that he had not called out once during the first week, but this week he had not been doing so well . . . I asked if the letter had been sent to his mother after the first week. The class teacher replied that no, this had not been as she had given him lots of extra time to complete his art and science work.

Whilst discussing the good reports she had received about the child the previous week, the Head restated her concern over the class teacher's management problems. I mentioned that it was unfortunate that the class teacher had not fulfilled her side of the contract. The Head immediately arranged for a letter to be typed, gave it to the child adding her own congratulations to him for his success. I am certain that her prompt action had the effect of making him feel it had been a worthwhile exercise. He said he thought it would be a good idea to re-negotiate and work on something else next term. He reported that his mother was really pleased with him.

INTERPRETING THE DATA

Although the above behaviour is clearly functional and is easy to interpret, other incidents may be more difficult to understand. In particular, it is often difficult to apply logical analysis to the behaviour of a child who is functioning at a profoundly disabled level. In a home setting, structured observation has led to the following analysis of the possible functions of a young child's hair-pulling and pinching. L. P. writes:

It has become a little clearer why T. may present challenging behaviour.

Boredom
Although it happens at other times, T.'s challenging behaviour mostly happens when the rest of the family are relaxing and chatting together, or watching television. On some of these occasions there is very little for T. to do, except to use the family (and their hair) as playthings.

Attention
Pulling hair and nipping is effective in getting a reaction and T. has learned this. It usually results in a shout, or someone crying, or even a smacked hand. This reaction may be more interesting to the child than just sitting and watching – he has caused something to happen and changed his environment. T. is getting social reinforcement for his behaviour, the antecedents are 'nothing much happening, nobody noticing me'.

Sensory feedback
The behaviour started because of T.'s fascination for long silky hair. He has always enjoyed stroking and flicking it, especially his mother's and sister's hair. They have never really discouraged it as it is a pleasurable experience for them too. Unfortunately, it now escalates into pulling and nipping, especially if T. is in his usual (favoured) position facing them on their laps.

Lack of communication

T. has no other way of saying 'I am bored', 'look at me', or 'give me something'. He has discovered gradually that his nipping and other challenging behaviours get results, they fulfil a communicative function. From observation, T. sometimes banged his head on a door, when he seemed to want to go in or out, e.g., when he wanted to be in the kitchen where his mother was cooking.

Escape/Annoyance

T. has learned that his family do not like having their hair pulled or being pinched. Sometimes he seems to use it if he is being asked to do something that he does not want to do (e.g., getting out of the car, getting dressed). He uses it as a way of opting out.

L. P. offers the following realistic and sensitive approach to intervention in a family setting:

I was concerned that much of our observations were rather subjective, but the information collected was valuable to all of us. We all agreed that we could effect some changes fairly quickly which would help the situation and put in place some longer term strategies. The family and I were excited about the observations we had made. They had never looked at T.'s behaviour in this 'structured' way, and they could see immediately that there were things that they could do. However, we agreed that before we considered any intervention, a few ground rules had to be considered:

- Any intervention must be practical, the family must be able to cope with it.
- Everyone must agree to the forms of intervention chosen and be willing to co-operate.
- Any strategies chosen should be gentle, aversive only in the sense that T.'s challenging behaviours will offer him no rewards.
- There will be a strong emphasis on offering him alternative ways of getting these results.
- There are three other children in the family, their needs must be considered. The family must work out how much time can be reasonably devoted to any skills teaching plan.
- School will be involved in the intervention plan, and will be kept informed of progress.
- Some goals will be long term, but these can be broken down into smaller steps, and will be reviewed at regular intervals.
- Our aim was to change some of T.'s behaviours, but not to change T.

A summary of L. P.'s proposed intervention shows an approach which is both practical and well conceived:

We worked out a weekly timetable. We identified the 'difficult' times, one of which was after tea and before T.'s bedtime, when he was bored. This was a time when mum felt she would like to sit with T. for 10–15 minutes and teach him something. The completed PVCS (Pre-Verbal Communication Schedule, Kiernan and Reid, 1987) indicated that T. has many communicative strengths, but his challenging behaviours seemed to represent a powerful agent for denial, showing needs, preferences, etc. The way forward seemed to teach him to use other forms of (more appropriate) communicative behaviour, whilst reducing the efficiency of his present (less appropriate) behaviours. The three strands of his intervention were:

(a) to provide him with more opportunities for choice–making by encouraging him to ask for preferred objects, activities, etc. by 1) pointing to the real objects (which are present), and 2) using Makaton Symbols to request objects (not present).

(b) to enable him to manage his free time better by widening his repertoire of toys and teaching him the skills needed to play with these toys.

(c) to reduce the opportunities when T. can pull hair. Family members will initially tie their hair up during difficult periods, discourage hair touching and redirect his attention to toys which offer the child strong tactile stimulation.

J. P. discusses his intervention for a child who shows physical aggression. His observations of the child revealed three distinct stages of disturbance: 1) a gradual build up of temper and frustration, 2) the child's physical aggression to peers and staff, in the form of punching, kicking and biting, and 3) the child's emotional breakdown, i.e., extreme episodes of crying, remorse and attempts to achieve solace. J. P. writes:

Earlier, an emergency contingency plan was described which involved a mild form of restraint of O. to prevent injury to other children and members of staff. However, what is really needed is a preventative strategy which could be implemented in the first phase of O.'s disturbance, something which would defuse the situation and hopefully reduce the need to use the emergency contingency. The following preventative strategies are to be tried.

An early warning system
Our observations indicate that one of the most stressful times for O. is when activity is drawing to a close and another is about to begin. O. is often taken by surprise in these transitional periods and he is often not ready to finish the activity in which he is involved. So, as change over points of the day are approaching, staff will give O. clear warnings that activities are to finish. O. uses Makaton signs, so adults will use the sign for 'finish' as a visual clue when they speak (thumbs spiralling slowly inwards towards the body). He needs to be informed in good time about finishing an activity, and warned that there will be a lot of movement in the class (something that O. finds upsetting). In addition to being informed about the approaching termination of the activity, O. is to be told what he will be doing next. Again, Makaton signs will be used with speech, and Makaton symbols will be used experimentally to offer further reinforcement.

New experiences

If O. is to be involved in a new or irregular experience such as a school outing, he needs to be thoroughly prepared for it, similar to the early warning system above. This preparation would involve discussion, showing photographs, pictures, even videos if feasible.

Developing communication

We cannot be certain that O.'s limited expressive communication is a reason in itself for the challenging behaviour which he sometimes presents, but there is little doubt that it is a contributory factor to the escalation of his temper tantrums prior to his physical outbursts. As well as giving O. clear verbal and visual clues to the structure of the day, O. will be encouraged to use signs and symbols to choose some of his activities, so he has some control over the sequence of part of his day. At the beginning of each day, O. will be involved in making a timetable of the day's main events using Makaton symbols.

WHOLE-SCHOOL APPROACHES TO MANAGING BEHAVIOUR

F. F. writes about the need continually to monitor and evaluate an individual behaviour management programme. However, having established that a particular intervention programme has been successful in reducing a child's challenging behaviour, F. F. states that its continued use is still not without its problems:

In general, the behaviour management programme for N. works well in the base-room where the staff have been committed to the strategies offered for intervention. There is a need to constantly monitor and assess the effectiveness of the school's policy and where it is not working to challenge inconsistencies and attitudes that prevent it from operating effectively. This is slow work, but the responsibility to diminish distressful and challenging behaviours must surely lie on the school's shoulders . . . A whole-school approach towards working positively with students who present challenging behaviour is critical. There should be a fundamental belief in the principle of 'ownership', that is, that staff should enable each other, and students, to cope effectively with challenging behaviours and any negative attitudes relating to them. This last point is perhaps the most difficult and burning issue in the daily practice of managing challenging behaviours; how to turn around what are often quite negative, entrenched attitudes, thus promoting a more healthy, stimulating and safe environment where real positive change can take place.

Similarly, in ordinary schools, the behaviour policy must be owned by all the teachers as well as the pupils, and differences in interpretation acknowledged in an environment where disruptive behaviour is not simply decontextualised:

Sometimes it is difficult to deal with behaviour problems. At the start of the academic year I try to get a good understanding of what is happening in each class, the students' age, ability, their interests and needs, in order to develop a good relationship with the students and to help me deal more effectively with behavioural problems when they arise . . . I think that, irrespective of pupils' home background, the school can be a key factor in determining whether certain pupils are being 'disruptive' or not . . . But it is very difficult to define disruption or to say which pupils commit disruptive acts because what can be regarded as disruptive behaviour by me for example can be required practice for another teacher . . . Some classroom confrontations between students and teachers can be caused because of small incidents which are not dealt with on time and the escalation of such incidents could cause bigger problems. Such escalation can be caused either by the students or the teacher. As an example I would say that some teachers, without realising, can be reinforcing unwanted behaviour in the classroom. Some pupils for example like to provoke the teacher by talking, arriving late, not bringing the text books etc. If the teacher gets angry, . . . with negative comments towards the student, they enjoy this situation because at that moment they are taking control . . . I know of a case of a 14 year old boy who has a reputation at school of being disruptive, aggressive and very difficult to manage. When he was in Year 7 he had an incident with a teacher where he reacted with very bad language and several threats. According to what he says, he was provoked by the teacher when she accused him of making noises all the time and disrupting other pupils. From that moment on she always picked on him for any little misdemeanour. As a result he has lost confidence in his teachers . . .

Disruptive behaviour and its causes are ecological and can be due to personal factors, school factors and social factors. Disruptive behaviour can be the result of the interaction between the person involved and the setting . . . I would say that behaviour can be very flexible according to different settings, and we as teachers cannot generalise because of certain behaviour patterns of a child in the school setting. (P. P.)

The following account places the difficult behaviour of a young child in a number of concentric ecosystemic contexts (Bronfenbrenner, 1979): the teacher describes how an early attempt to resolve the problem without reference to personal and social factors as well as to the school situation was succeeded by a more effective intervention in which all the relevant people were involved, with appropriate resource to a clear whole-school policy:

Peter is a very lively (possibly 'hyperactive') four and a half year old. He comes from a close knit Caribbean family. Both his parents are very caring and take a keen interest in their children's education. There are three children in the family, of which Peter is the eldest. The second child has Down's Syndrome, and was very ill during the first year of life, spending long periods in hospital. During this time Peter was looked after by different relatives, spending a great deal of time away from his parents. At the age of three years Peter was diagnosed by his parents and Health Visitor as being retarded in his speech, and having social and emotional difficulties. He was referred to a Local Authority Day Nursery, where he was given specialist help from a Speech Therapist, and a qualified Special Needs teacher. Both professionals worked closely with Peter's mother devising a work plan which Peter would do at the nursery, and which would be continued at home. Peter made very good progress, therefore it was felt that he would not require 'statementing' as a 'special needs' child, when transferring to Primary School. However Peter's mother did inform the Head of the School, of Peter's immaturity, and that he still needed help with his speech, and would require firm but fair discipline in order to settle satisfactorily into the new environment.

Throughout my (limited) observation of Peter in the classroom, I found him to be very alert, talkative (although his speech was sometimes garbled because he tried to speak too quickly) and very keen to be involved in all the activities. He tended to rush from one activity to another, and had to be constantly reminded by the teacher to settle down. His attention span was relatively short, which adversely affected the rate at which he was learning reading, writing and number skills (the core curriculum). He appeared to be less disruptive when playing with the construction toys or doing art work. However with 1 to 1 tuition he was able to cope with the more 'academic' activities. During my second visit, I noticed that Peter was being particularly disruptive. He became very agitated, when some of the children began mimicking his speech. He then began shouting loudly, which prompted the nursery assistant to intervene. She tried to remove Peter from the others, whilst attempting to remove a pencil from him. Peter swung his arm away from her, and accidentally hit another child in the face with the point of the pencil. The child became hysterical and Peter was forcefully taken from the room by the class teacher, and frog marched to the Headteacher's office. At this point the School's disciplinary process took effect.

The school's policy on Discipline as stated in its 1991/92 Handbook suggests that: 'Praise is perhaps more important than punishment, in the maintenance of good discipline. We should take every opportunity that presents itself to offer encouragement and praise to each child.' This policy statement echoes many of the examples of the behaviour policies used by 'good schools' included in Appendix F3 of the Elton Report 1989 (p. 286). Although the Report whole-heartedly recommends these policies, it also recommends by contrast, in R23, p. 26, that schools should strike a 'healthy balance between "Rewards and Punishments", in spite of its own recognition of the negative effects of punishment' (para 4.43, p. 98). In emphasising a system of rewards rather than punitive measures, the school has certificates and stickers for good conduct, good work, for being helpful etc. Periodically the names of children who gain these certificates is mentioned in Assembly. The disciplinary procedures of the school are as follows:

(1) Any discipline problems should first be dealt with in the classroom by the class teacher. If the problem cannot be resolved by the class teacher, then it is referred to the Deputy Head and finally the Headteacher.

(2) If the matter is considered to be extremely serious (no elaboration of what constitutes 'serious' behaviour), then parents are informed in writing, or asked to discuss the matter face to face, with the headteacher.

(3) Other strategies which may then be employed to resolve serious behavioural problems include the use of 'Daily Report Cards' (i.e. the pupil reports daily to the Deputy Head) and Home-school Liaison Book where the child's behaviour is monitored and recorded by the class teacher, headteacher and the parent.

(4) In extreme cases the child may be excluded from school for a limited period.

The handbook includes a section on punishment under which it reminds staff that corporal punishment in schools was banned by the 1986 Education Act. It states further that if it is necessary to punish a child, the staff may use whatever punishment seems appropriate within certain parameters:

Children may only be kept in at playtimes or lunchtimes under supervision, and not after school.

Children should not be left outside the classroom door.

Avoid using corporate punishment, e.g. everyone is punished for one child's misbehaviour.

Staff should not make threats which they are not prepared to act upon.

The writer notes that this advice, while appearing to sanction 'punishment', is not forthcoming about what kind of punishment is acceptable, although it is specific about what is not. 'It therefore relies upon the resourcefulness of the class teacher to cope when faced, daily, with intractable children':

In Peter's case the school adopted intervention strategies to try and solve the problem behaviour, based initially on reacting to the effects of the bad behaviour he displayed, and without the involvement of other parties in the probable cause and solution of the problem i.e. the other children in the class (especially those who were mimicking Peter), his parents (who foresaw Peter would have difficulties in adjusting to school life, and wanted to work closely with the teachers to try and overcome those difficulties), the Support Agencies (The LEA's Special Needs Adviser, the Health visitor, Speech Therapist, all of whom had provided help for Peter in the past). The class teacher, deciding that the incident was too serious to be resolved in the classroom, referred the matter to the Headteacher. Discussions between the class teacher and the Head in the absence of the parents and without their knowledge, concluded that Peter's behaviour would be monitored/recorded daily, and that he would spend some time in another classroom, with a senior member of staff.

Peter's parents were not informed of this strategy for some two weeks after the decision was taken, during which time Peter's behaviour worsened.

By not recognising the contributory environmental factors which affected Peter's behaviour, and by failing to involve all parties in the interactions surrounding the problem, the school's intervention strategies exacerbated Peter's problems, angered and alienated his parents rather than providing a workable solution. However when Peter's mother was informed of the situation by the Head and the Class Teacher (both of whom apologised for not informing her earlier) she made a special effort to gain support from other agencies outside the school. A programme was designed to meet Peter's needs by the Headteacher, the class teacher and the special needs adviser in consultation with Peter's mother. Peter now receives extra help with his reading and speech. Any behaviour is dealt with in the classroom and reported to his mother each day. He goes home for lunch, which provides a calming effect on his behaviour during the afternoon.

The roles played by the key participants, the class teacher, the headteacher and the parents and support agencies, were fundamental in identifying the cause of Peter's behaviour problems and providing practical solutions. (P. R.)

Here is neatly demonstrated that 'whole-school policies' and written guidelines are useless unless understood and applied: Peter's problems could not be addressed where the class teacher was left with only the vaguest of guidelines about what was appropriate action. One wonders if the teacher recently reported as having taped a child's mouth for talking too much was given any clearer guidelines on rewards and punishments.

Finally, concerns are often expressed about the degree to which all staff understand and can apply agreed rules of management:

I was teaching GCSE Child care to a class of Year 11 students (all girls) and a dispute arose about where three students wished to sit in the class. They wanted to sit in the dining alcove of the Home Economics room, out of sight, and I wanted them to sit in the main body of the room; I was informed that Mrs H. always let them sit there. After a colourful dispute, in which the girls refused to move, I found myself having to seek the assistance of the deputy head (female) who told me that the ringleader of the girls had a 'difficult' background. She then told the girls that they could stay where they were. I am aware that I did not handle the situation well; I was unable to take the long view and use strategies to defuse the situation. However, the complete lack of support from a senior teacher meant that I had no back-up in dealing with the class for the rest of the term. (P. Q.)

I would like to see a great deal more contact with parents, bringing them in at the beginning of the problem to enlist their support and help at home rather than leaving things until they have escalated almost out of control and instead of consultation there is confrontation. There is also still the feeling that the problem should be shifted onto somone else's shoulders – the teacher has enough to cope with, dealing with 30 odd children in the class. There is usually a feeling of relief if a child is excluded rather than examining the reasons for the failure of the school to deal with the problem. There is also a tendency for classes to get labelled and while there are attempts to mix them up the label still tends to stick. (L. G.)

The staff are not together in ensuring that the rules are always adhered to. (L. G.)

Many of the staff attend courses on dealing with behaviour problems, working with outside agencies and helping children with special needs in class but little time is given for them to report back to the rest of their colleagues and perhaps introduce some new ideas into the school. I would like to see this done on a much more formal basis with ideas being discussed among the staff and then studies being carried out and monitored. (L. G.)

CONCLUSION

Despite errors and false starts, there is an overriding feeling of optimism permeating the extracts in this chapter. The challenging behaviour of children with severe learning difficulties is seen to be complex, but not unfathomable. Some of the examples show how children's difficulties should be viewed from outside the child – and how we should critically examine both the learning environments that we provide for our children and our own professional practice. We have learned much about challenging behaviour from recent research and the painstaking work done in analysing learning and social situations in SLD classrooms is mirrored in other settings to help us to understand emotional and behavioural difficulties. (It is sad to see how some research centres like Hilda Lewis House, where much of our understanding of self-injurious behaviour originated, have been closed because of Health Service cutbacks.) It is to the credit of the teaching profession that children who present serious challenging behaviour, including those with severe learning difficulties, remain in our schools. For many of them, it will be the best years of their lives. Life after school is not so rosy.

SECTION 5
How Teachers Learn

10

Teachers and Professional Development

The Code of Practice suggested that a school's SEN policy should 'describe plans for the in-service training and professional development of staff to help them work effectively with pupils with special educational needs' (para 2:26). The Code goes on to state that 'The SEN in-service training policy should be part of the school's development plan and should, where appropriate, cover the needs of non-teaching assistants and other staff' (para 2:26). To many this guidance may appear to be unremarkable; indeed it is probably representative of what schools have been doing for a good many years.

But the guidance assumes a problematic nature when it is placed in the context of developments in both initial teacher education (ITE) and in the broader framework of reductions in funds available to finance in-service training (INSET) and continuing professional development (CPD). This concluding chapter begins with a brief examination of the changes in ITE in general, outlining their impact on the future professional development of newly qualified teachers (NQTs). The nature of SEN provision within ITE is then looked at, and the effects on the CPD of teachers involved in SEN completes the scene-setting.

There has been a noticeable shift in the way in which ITE has been organised since 1988. A student's school experience was previously obtained alongside considerable practice-related study within university departments of education, a strategy reliant upon a series of largely *ad hoc* relationships between these departments and schools (McCulloch, 1993). Recently, however, there has been a move towards school-based training (HMI, 1991), prompted at least in part by the right-wing viewpoint that 'present patterns of training help to perpetuate a damagingly "progressive" educational establishment, and so contribute significantly to low standards in the schools' (Edwards, 1992). In consequence, since Circular 9/92 (DfE, 1992), ITE courses have been required to implement plans to raise the percentage of school-based content to a minimum of two-thirds.

There have also been changes in the content and pedagogy of ITE courses (Furlong, 1992). In part this adjustment has been required in order to provide adequate coverage of the National Curriculum and the heavier emphasis being placed upon subject studies in ITE courses since 1988. As a result student-teachers now have little time for 'reflection', given official demands for subject-knowledge, based upon the principles of 'technical rationalism' (Carr and Kemmis, 1986). The prevailing view, vigorously promoted by recent government circulars, and by the implementation of the National Curriculum itself, has been that the key to the effective 'training' is to be found in providing student teachers with a firm grasp of the academic disciplines (Lawlor, 1990). This is an example of the move away from a critical and humanistic approach in ITE to one based upon technical rationality (Hargreaves, 1994), in which teacher education is viewed as 'narrowly functional, emphasising only what will be professionally useful to teachers' (Furlong, 1992). Moreover, the shift towards a model of ITE which is based upon a series of competencies (McNamara, 1992) has fulfilled the ideological requirements of the reformers of the so-called New Right, with the result that 'During the 1980s, teacher education was framed more by the needs of capitalism than by the principles of democracy, to the detriment of the latter. This is a reversal of what occurred in the 1970s when there had been a growth of reflective practice' (Hartley, 1991).

Reflective practice has been defined, and used, in many ways. A typical strategy, based upon the work of Schon (1983, 1987) identifies three approaches which draw upon a wide range of contexts and means of working with recalled 'facts'. In them a tutor would typically engage a student (or coach, as Schon would say) in the task of 'enquiring consciously into his/her own and each other's changing understandings' (Fish et al., 1991). Doing this is a time-consuming and intensive activity, but it gained in popularity in ITE during the 1970s and early 1980s.

The vociferous demands of the 'New Right' significantly influenced the approach of central goverment towards teacher education practices, which were increasingly portrayed as permissive, or even dangerous (Lawlor, 1990). Subsequently, institutions providing ITE had to review their approaches and content, in order to meet requirements laid out by the government via the Council for Accreditation of Teacher Education (CATE). In these there is an emphasis on 'outputs', measured as 'competencies', rather than processes (Benton, 1990). Hill (1994) has caustically summarised this situation, noting that 'Critical issues are being replaced by detheorised, "how to", practical courses. The Conservative intention is to restrict ITE courses to a non-critical instruction and training in how to "deliver", uncritically, the Conservative National Curriculum.'

SPECIAL NEEDS IN ITE AND INSET

This shift in philosophy and organisation has had a disastrous effect on those parts of ITE courses which concern SEN. The Warnock Report (1978) had recognised that an SEN component should be included in all ITE courses and since 1984 the provision of such a core element has been essential for the accreditation of ITE courses (DES, 1984). Validating this type of provision, Mittler (1993) stated that 'The successful education of children with special educational needs in ordinary schools depends on all teachers having a basic core of relevant information, knowledge and skills, as well as positive attitudes to the education of such children'. This approach has subsequently received official acknowledgement in Circular 9/92, which states that newly qualified teachers (NQTs) should demonstrate the competence to 'recognise diversity of talent, including that of gifted pupils' and to 'identify special educational needs or learning difficulties' (DfE, 1992).

The overriding demand for technical competence and subject-knowledge, together with the lack of time for students to consider their forthcoming role in relation to SEN, as a result of the move towards predominantly school-based training, has now created a crisis in ITE (Aubrey, 1994). Thus, 'Concern has been expressed by practitioners about the pressures on the beginning teacher's programme of professional development. In England and Wales the National Curriculum is creating significant time demands . . . The fear is that the amount of time for special educational needs issues will decline' (CNAA, 1991). One notable response to this situation has been for many training institutions to opt for a process of 'permeation', in which SEN matters are subsumed within each element of training and become the responsibility of all tutors within an ITE team. Whilst this approach has gone some way to enabling all students to obtain at least some SEN information there are, as Mittler has noted, considerable difficulties in its implementation. These include the variable quality of provision from one tutor to the next, the acceptance by course teams of the intrinsic need to make SEN matters a continued point of emphasis, and, importantly, the concern that 'permeation is by its very nature invisible and therefore difficult to monitor' (Mittler, 1993).

The current picture is therefore one of considerable uncertainty, with little evidence forthcoming that one approach to ITE is more successful than another. As Thomas (1993) has indicated,

the success of higher education training institutions in providing appropriate preparation for pre-service teachers to meet special needs has been variable. They have found themselves, for a variety of reasons, coping with this problem through either ghetto-izing special needs into strictly cabined timetable slots . . . or relying on a diffusion model in which the quality control over subject specialist tutors' input was at best partial and at worse, non existent. (p. 113)

The changes described above, both to general ITE provision and to SEN in particular, have had profound implications for INSET and the CPD of serving teachers. Commenting on the demise of full-time SEN courses and other INSET opportunities, Carpenter and Bovair (1990) state that 'This narrowing of the range of professional development opportunities for teachers is deeply worrying . . . Already the area of severe learning difficulties (SLD) is beginning to feel the pinch.' Nor is this expression of concern anything new. Mittler (1993), for example, stridently argued that in the 'New Look' in INSET 'Special needs staff neither expect nor receive positive discrimination at the expense of their colleagues but what is the point of being told that you are a high priority when you see no sign of it in the resources available for you to do your job'.

The failure to adequately resource INSET and CPD in SEN has, of course, been a long-running educational soap opera. There is little doubt that many teachers involved in SEN become intensely frustrated at this situation which can lead for some to 'a mood of professional depression . . . closely related to clinical depression – a feeling of inertia and helplessness, a conviction that all is for the worst in the worst of all possible worlds and that there is nothing to be done except to carry on as best one can' (Mittler, 1993).

The substance of this chapter suggests that not only are many teachers engaged in SEN work able to 'carry on', but they are doing so in spite of increasingly unpromising financial arrangements for INSET and CPD. In one sense, therefore, the teachers' comments provided as evidence of this commitment and spirit are indicative of their overall attitude to the work that they do. Judge for yourself . . .

SEN has, since the 1981 Act, assumed the status of a bona-fide sub-division of education as whole – irrespective of the developing view that teachers should now dispense with the term 'special educational needs' and utilise integrationist terms like 'inclusivity'. Whatever our views on the matter, the pressures on teachers to meet individual needs, whilst at the same time responding to copious policy directives from central government, has resulted in what may be seen as a 'core' of INSET activities for SEN, resulting in the professional development of those involved.

Gross (1993) has provided one example of what the range of issues might be. Apart from work devoted to meeting the needs of groups of children who have MLD, EBD or SLD (whether or not they are statemented), a series of additional matters need to be addressed. Some of these are used in the extracts contained in this chapter to illustrate the dynamics, and the accompanying tensions, of this kind of professional activity.

But prior to considering the ways in which teachers have managed to deal with these dilemmas it is important to recognise that INSET, both in the way in which it is 'delivered' and in its content, has incorporated many of the features of the new paradigm in learning. These have been considered in detail by Whitaker (1995). For the contextual purposes of this chapter, a number of these need to be highlighted as they underpin, either explicitly or implicitly, the responses of the teachers to this aspect of their development.

Firstly, INSET activity has, in the last dozen or so years, incorporated flexible structures, varied starting points and mixed learning experiences. Teachers, as a professional body, are not a uniform collection of machine-produced units, all with the same, collective experience and background. Their professional development via INSET should therefore offer opportunities to make use of this variety. A number of our contributing teachers have, in the extracts contained in this chapter, considered this to be the single most valuable aspect of contemporary INSET provision.

A second characteristic of current INSET development is that, in recognising the breadth of experience that teachers possess, the participants assume a position of equal status. It is worth remembering that Holt's (1971) observations, concerning the failure of some children to learn, can be applied equally to teachers taking part in INSET activities. As Holt remarked, 'the child comes to feel that learning is a passive process, something that someone else does to you, instead of something that you do for yourself'. The same passivity can be generated when teachers themselves are not recognised as experts within their field.

Finally, it is particularly noteworthy that INSET provision has traditionally recognised the importance of practical applications of theory. In recent years considerable criticism has been levelled at INSET provided by university departments. This has usually been by non-participants, and often driven by ideological notions that such departments were intent on subverting, rather than supporting, government policy. In the work that we have done, and continue to do, with teachers on masters and diploma courses it is clear that most of the participants recognise the importance of striking a balance between the two. Neither is indispensable.

For many teachers the success of an INSET session is in a large part judged by the opportunities it offers for them to work collectively with colleagues from other types of schools and other areas. Their comments, in evaluation of many courses, reflect an opinion that is probably generalisable: INSET provision can become narrow and introspective if it relies predominantly on input from a designated person from the school and that of its teachers. Even where external 'facilitators' are used, this situation remains apparent. But such retrogressive developments are hardly surprising, given the reduction in funding for INSET in SEN which we have previously noted. The evidence provided by many of the teachers in this study bears witness to this. R. R., for example, notes that 'The process of meeting and discussing with colleagues from other SLD schools and the process of practical and theoretical assignments and the wide reading has helped me professionally.'

Contemporary INSET arrangements, especially when they are able to gather together a wide range of teachers from different backgrounds, strive to strike a balance between theory and practice, and use 'reflection' as an integral part of this process. Wherever this activity is based this approach, almost by definition, requires time and space to allow thinking to take place.

R. R. develops this theme by looking back on the professional development she has been undertaking. She argues that her reasons for starting a formal course of study (which leads to a diploma or masters degree) were quite different from the outcomes resulting from a period of extensive reflection. Her view is that:

When I started the course I wanted 'ideas' about what to do with these students. I hadn't considered the possibility of me developing as I hadn't really seen the link between me and my students and that through me developing I would bring a breadth and richness to the school. When I first started teaching I thought there was only one way to do everything. Now I feel at times I have raised more problems [and] now I see education in a much broader way than before. In the future I would ensure, encourage INSET in whatever form for staff. Teachers need time to reflect, then put it into action.

But it is also the case that by, engaging in INSET as a means of CPD the role of many teachers involved in SEN work begins to change. Some commentators have argued that the contemporary SEN teacher is more of a consultant (Dyson, 1990), and this view would appear to be borne out by the involvement of such teachers as INSET providers. Thus, R. R. observes that:

I have become a specialist. I was very concerned about my lack of knowledge and understanding of the PMLD students . . . three and a half years on I am a resource in school who leads sessions for this group and chairs regular meetings for other staff over concerns for the PMLD students.

These sentiments indicate an encouraging advance in the way in which SEN teachers view their role in INSET. They are, increasingly, moving from being simply the provided-for to becoming providers in their own right. This introduces them to some of the dilemmas consistently found in INSET and CPD, but the opportunities for success remain considerable.

T. T. is able to provide an extended commentary, which encompasses both the threats and the opportunities presented to teachers who have the opportunity to work in this way:

The school I work in has a range of teachers who use a variety of approaches. The overriding approach seems to be behaviourist. When I first started I found the approach quite difficult to adopt because my natural instinct was to be more interactive with students and I wanted to have more fun with them! During my course I listened to two guest speakers, Dave Hewitt and Melanie Nind. It was the most refreshing and relieving experience I have had in my professional career. I was so delighted to listen to their intensive interaction techniques and wanted to put them into practice immediately. It gave me the confidence and empowered me to use an approach that I really believed in. It was met with some cynicism at work so I arranged to have Dave Hewitt come to the school for an in-service training day. He was popular and people accepted his methods. Very soon after he left many conflicts arose and I realised that there were many people who found this challenge to their own approach very unnerving. I invited Dave Hewitt back to actually work with our students. He worked very successfully with one boy and this helped raise people's awareness.

It is also refreshing that many of the teachers who work in this way provide reassuring insights into the difficulties posed in managing such activities, where a wide range of viewpoints need to be accommodated. W. L., for example, is keen to stress a view, probably shared by many INSET providers, that

The strong idealists are far easier to debate with than those who have let lethargy creep in, have no real ideologies and have become resistant to change. These are the teachers who are often hostile to those undertaking professional development courses.

The authors of this volume are deeply empathic of these sentiments, having, from time to time, experienced the problem of working with 'pressed men' on 'Baker Days'. Vigorous professional debate, however oppositional the participants appear to be, has its place in reflection, as it serves as a trigger for thinking about why it is that we work in the way we do. Passivity, in this respect, represents the greater danger, as does the colleague who, by dint of experiences which tell him 'we have always done it this way', feels that there is little more to be learnt. For, as H. H. maintains, 'In some ways it becomes more evident that the more you learn the less you seem to know. I feel strongly that once a teacher thinks s/he knows everything s/he should leave the profession.'

Thankfully, however, a more expansive view concerning the value of INSET and CPD prevails within the profession. We have heard it argued that SEN teachers resemble Type A, rather than Type B people, in that they are more open to change (although they can at times be irascible and disorganised . . . !). They display, therefore, considerable fortitude and maintain enthusiasm for their own CPD even at times when INSET opportunities seem to be restricted by time and money. The remarks of two of our contributors bear witness to this state of affairs:

I have never analysed my working week in any detail before or really given any to reflective thought . . . It's very much an instinctive feel for the work which encompasses intuitive skills plus a full time teaching commitment. This has been a frantic week – and amazingly tiring. The time-management of the first three days was dreadful and I've now become more aware of staggering late-night meetings. Thursday's event brought a lighter touch to the week but as I had to drive to Richmond after school, for my course, that meant four consecutive late nights, compounded by the angst on Friday afternoon . . . (G. E.)

I have found coming back to study two nights each week, on top of a full-time teaching post in a very active school, very hectic. You are usually arriving from a meeting at school, working with a pupil, solving a problem and then straight into a lecture. At least the coffee shop is open before we start now. (V. V.)

The previous two commentaries point to the fact that many teachers have to engage in INSET and maintain their own professional development in a society which is frequently ambivalent about the value of such work and in which many seek to de-professionalise teaching by reducing it to a mechanical series of competencies and functions. In this climate, B. B., in summarising one phase of her own INSET involvement, maintains that it has given her, and SEN teachers like her, the 'confidence to fight your corner and understand'.

Given the state of affairs described above, it may be viewed as remarkable to the casual observer, therefore, that energy remains to attend to critical thinking and reflection. But there is abundant evidence that this type of analysis is forthcoming. It represents one way in which INSET leads to professional development at a very personal level. The following extracts are provided as valedictions of the work that teachers do in this aspect of their professional lives. Each comment is a summation of what teachers see as the principal, interrelated purposes behind such work.

Firstly, its likely effect on all the children that they teach or come into contact with, but especially on those who have SEN. It remains a feature of many INSET programmes offered by universities or other organisations that there will always be those participants who follow a single session, or perhaps a module comprising a number of sessions, without ever wishing to proceed to a formal qualification. In other words the drive is for personal enhancement and enrichment, in order to provide a more effective learning experience for the children. INSET, in this way, is about awareness-raising at a general level. Thus, W. L., working in a mainstream school, notes that

Now life – the real world began. I was forced to look at where these children really are as opposed to where I would like them to be. [Theirs was a world of] busy classrooms with teachers stressed by the National Curriculum, with little or no access to specialist-trained teachers. This was a dilemma – how to combine the theory with the practice: what was feasible?

A similar process was recorded by T. T., a teacher in a special school, who outlines the overlap between the development of a clearer sense of 'place' for someone working in a very discrete aspect of education:

When I first started working in a school for children with SLD I had never met anyone who had profound and multiple learning difficulties. I felt very anxious and inadequate when I did and had no effective way of communicating with them and certainly did not know how to effectively meet their needs. I needed to rely upon intuition and my 'caring' abilities.

But it goes without saying that a principal reason for involvement in INSET is the wish of teachers to extend their existing skills and to clarify their own thinking about aspects of SEN work which are contentious, topical or requiring enhancement in order that practice can be refined. Often this resulted in practical action within school, as V. Q. points out:

I have been able to look more critically at my role as coordinator of special needs . . . My first aim will be to set up a designated time each half term when I can get together with class teachers to plan differentiation and set individual targets.

Our contributors also remind us that they see part of their role as that of an instigator of discussion and ultimately that of a change-agent within their school. Thirdly, then, many of these teachers express the hope that, in developing their own skills and insights, they might influence the thinking and practice of their colleagues, as the following comments from two teachers working in special schools suggest:

I would hope that my other colleagues might find the project sufficiently interesting to form the basis of a discussion in one of the curriculum meetings at school. (Z. R.)

Clearly if targets such as these [National Curriculum Attainment Targets] were to be included in any school development plan there would be implications for staff training and in this sense it may be possible for the new assessment system to assist in the identification of staff training needs. Again, within my own school although the Programmes of Study may well be used to identify areas of need with regard to staff training the assessment process is unlikely to make any significant contribution. (W. S.)

And finally, it is readily apparent that many teachers are conscious that INSET will have a major impact on developments in the school as a whole, both in a direct, practical way, by helping to maintain and extend the expertise of those working with children who have SEN, and by ensuring that the morale and commitment of these teachers is maintained in times of increasing official scrutiny:

The school development plan is currently looking at various areas where the staff feel they are weakest and INSET is being planned for those areas. (L. G.)

Added to the stress of the inspection (OFSTED) all children in both the primary and secondary departments have been on school journey this year – an admirable achievement – but the cost of the combination has led to tiredness and short tempers and, not surprisingly, low morale. All the planning in the world can't compensate for the ghastliness of having one's teaching skills, record keeping and planning gone through with a fine tooth comb, no amount of platitudes or praise after the event can make up for the feelings of abject terror that an inspection seems to generate, despite the firm belief that both you and your fantastic staff really have worked and are working in the best interests of the children. (G. E.)

CONCLUSION

In the opening two sections of this chapter we outlined some of the current difficulties facing both the participants in, and the providers of, INSET. We have noted the constant pressure placed on the profession in recent years to implement changes in general education as well as in generic special educational needs. Whilst it is currently fashionable to talk of 'inclusive education', such rhetoric can only be translated into reality by a body of professionals who have been given the opportunity to reformulate the codes, protocols and procedures that govern what happens to the child in school who has SEN. In support of such a measure our contributors appear to subscribe to the belief of one of their number, that in order to have any positive impact on the learning progress of children:

Teachers need to be aware of their own values, attitudes, beliefs, theories, strengths and weaknesses. (T. T.)

Conclusion

When we began to prepare this book we knew that we could draw upon a wide range of material from all the teachers who had worked with us on INSET courses. That we have completed our task with more than fifty contributors, some of whom are represented by substantial extracts, is a surprise to all of us.

The overwhelming impression we gain from the sum of all our work is that teachers in special education have maintained quality, in thinking, managing and teaching which is disproportionately large when compared to the esteem in which they are held by some within the educational establishment and by many outside of it. The extracts included here demonstrate conclusively the validity of the concept of the teacher-researcher.

Special education teachers are often more inventive than others, perhaps because they are allowed more autonomy in managing, teaching and designing curricula. But this autonomy is bought at the cost of low status, a heavy workload and poor career prospects. It is not without significance that only seven of our contributors are male, a percentage which echoes that on the courses themselves.

One of the characteristics of the work we have included is the degree to which the teachers have maintained a reflective stance, despite the fact that reflection, in the age of 'curriculum delivery', is now at a premium. The focus throughout has been on the learning needs of children, with a commitment to looking at children's problems with the curriculum and with life in school, and listening to them and their parents as they struggle to come to terms with them.

Students in initial training, who currently encounter special educational needs (SEN) as a 'permeated' focus, slipped in among the subject studies and the competences, begin their careers with little comprehension of the complexity of the SEN role. Now that these students are required to spend more time in schools, their programmes will need to include participation in teaching children with special educational needs, and contact with specialist teachers. This will help to temper the concentration on 'delivery' and competences with a countervailing emphasis on teaching as a *creative* activity. The SEN teacher is best placed to provide this.

An area of concern which has been uncovered through the selection process, is that of inter-professional collaboration. The few extracts which deal, for example, with teachers' contacts with educational psychologists, do not describe very happy relationships. Not that this is anybody's fault: the problem appears to be that 'consulting professionals' such as psychologists and therapists have their own work so constrained by time and extended by responsibilities that the space they have for collaborative work with teachers is very limited. If the system of referral and support promoted in the Code of Practice is to work successfully, multi-professional assessment must mean just that, not simply a relation between parents and teachers, but one in which the work of all those concerned is known and understood. Certainly, despite the consumerism which has become fashionable, parents and teachers appear to be able to relate to one another along a human dimension.

Again and again our contributors point out how the organisational and management aspects of their role are completed largely without any time allocation. Managers in industry with liaison responsibilities inside and outside their organisations would be astonished if their work had to be completed without any preparation or meeting time, and without access to secretarial or administrative support, or even a telephone. There is still too easy an assumption that a teacher is only concerned with face to face work in the classroom, and that other duties are minimal.

It is our contention that the special needs teacher, whether in the mainstream or in the special school, has a contribution to make to the education system as a whole which is far greater than their numbers indicate. This contribution remains relatively unacknowledged and undervalued (witness the numbers of newly appointed SENCOs who already have full-time classes and no non-contact time). It is our hope that this volume will help to redress the balance.

POSTSCRIPT

At time of going to press, we have received a copy of 'Innovatory Practice in Mainstream Schools for Special Educational Needs', published by DfE (1995). In view of the real innovation and real concern revealed by our contributors, we would argue that the claim that this official volume offers 'examples of creative and innovative approaches' to special education practice is hardly borne out by the content. In fact the use of the word 'innovatory' in the title is misleading, given the authors' summary view that 'many of the surface features of what we found could equally well have been found in the previous decade'.

Teachers working in schools frequently express the need to be provided with exemplars of good practice, not exhortations couched in generalities. It is unlikely that a hard-pressed classroom teacher will gain much sustenance from phrases like 'one school had adopted a thoroughgoing individual differences perspective' or that 'one coordinator saw the management of behaviour not in terms of controlling disruption, but of releasing and then channelling pupils' energies through appropriate teaching'. Starkly absent in this volume are detailed accounts of what works in classrooms, of what thinking has guided this practice and what future directions might be for child, teacher and school.

Critically, the issue of time management is virtually ignored, the authors merely satisfying themselves with the comforting statement that 'Given sufficient prioritisation of Special Needs, the creative management of resources, and the realisation that special needs issues are linked more generally to issues of teaching and learning for all, then the coordinator's role becomes not simply viable but integral to the development of the school' (p. 81). In various chapters of *this* book, there are detailed accounts of the role of the SENCO. The reader may profitably refer to them in the light of the quoted statement.

The DfE study, which according to its publicity is complementary to the SEN Code of Practice, suffers from some of the drawbacks of the Code itself. In particular, the Code similarly provides advice without a commensurate set of examples to illustrate its application. *What Teachers Do* has been designed to show how theory can realistically translate into practice.

References

Advisory Centre for Education (1994a) Preparing for the Code of Practice: Issues for Governors, *ACE Bulletin*, 58, March/April, pp. 9–12.

Advisory Centre for Education (1994b) Draft Code of Practice – ACE response, *ACE Bulletin*, 57, January/February, pp. 13–14.

Ager, A. (1989) Behavioural teaching strategies, *Mental Handicap*, 17, pp. 56–9.

Ainscow, M. (1990) Responding to individual needs, *British Journal of Special Education*, 3 (3).

Apple, M. (1986) *Teachers and Text: A Political Economy of Class and Gender Relations in Education*, Routledge & Kegan Paul, London.

Aubrey, C. (1994) A testing time for psychologists, in Sandow, S. (ed.) *Whose Special Need? Some Perceptions of Special Educational Needs*, Paul Chapman Publishing, London.

Aubrey, C. (1994) Who teaches the teachers?, *Special Children*, October, pp. 20–2.

Bangs, J. (1993) Support Services – Stability or Erosion? *British Journal of Special Education*, 20 (3), pp. 105–7.

Barton, L. (1991) Teachers under siege: a case of unmet needs, *Support for Learning*, 6 (1), pp. 3–8.

Bastiani, J. (1987) *Perspectives on home-school relations: Parents and Teachers*, Vol 1, NFER Nelson, Windsor.

Bastiani, J. (1993) Parents as partners, genuine progress or empty rhetoric, in Munn, P. (ed.) *Parents and schools: Customers, Managers or Partners*, Routledge, London.

Becker, H. (1970) *Sociological Work: Method and Substance*, Transaction Books, New Brunswick.

Bell, G., Stakes, R. and Taylor, G. (ed.) (1994) *Action Research, Special Needs and School Development*, David Fulton, London.

Bender, M. and Valletutti, P. (1982) *Teaching Functional Academics, a Curriculum Guide for Adolescents and Adults with Learning Problems*, University Park Press, Baltimore.

Benson, C. (1991) The science curriculum: an interactive approach, in Smith, B. (ed.) *Interactive Approaches to Teaching the Core Subjects*, Lame Duck Publishing, Bristol.

Benton, P. (ed.) (1990) *The Oxford Internship Scheme: Integration and Partnership in Initial Teacher Education*, Calouste Gulbenkian Foundation, London.

Best, R. (1991) Support Teaching in a Comprehensive School: Some Reflections on Current Practice, *Support for Teaching*, 6 (1).

Bines, H. (1989) Whole school policies at primary level, *British Journal of Special Education*, 16 (2), pp. 80–2.

Bines, H. (1993) Whole school policies in the new era, *British Journal of Special Education*, 20 (3), pp. 91–4.

Blenkin,G., Edwards, C. and Kelly, A. (1992) *Change and the Curriculum*, Paul Chapman, London.

Bluma, S., Shearer, M., Fishman, A. and Millward, J. (1976) *Portage Guide to Early Education Portage Project*, Wisconsin.

Booth, T. (1994) Continua or Chimera, *British Journal of Special Education*, 20 (3), pp. 91–4.

Booth, T. and Coulby, D. (eds.) (1987) *Producing and Reducing Disaffection*, Open University Press, Milton Keynes.

Borkowski, J. and Buchel, F, (1983) Learning and memory strategies in the mentally retarded, in *Cognitive Strategy Research: Psychological Foundations*, Springer-Verlag, New York.

Borkowski, J., Reid, M. and Kurtz, B. (1984) Metacognition and retardation: paradigmatic, theoretical, and applied perspectives, in Brooks, P., Sperber, R. and McCauley, C. (eds.) *Learning and Cognition in the Mentally Retarded*, Hillsdale, Lawrence Erlbaum Associates, New Jersey.

Bowe, R. and Ball, S. (1992) *Reforming Education and Changing Schools*, Routledge, London.

Bronfenbrenner, U. (1979) *The Ecology of Human Development*, Harvard University Press, Cambridge, Mass.

Brown, G. (1977) *Child Development*, Open Books, London.

Bruner, J. S. (1963) *The Process of Education*, Vintage Books, New York.

Buckley and Bird (1994) *Meeting the Educational Needs of Children with Down's Syndrome*, The Sarah Duffin Centre.

Bush, L. and Hill, T. (1993) The right to teach, the right to learn, *British Journal of Special Education*, 20 (1), pp. 4–6.

Butt, N. (1986) Implementing the whole school approach at secondary level, *Support for Learning*, 1 (4), pp. 10–15.

Butt, N. and Scott, E. (1994) Individual education programmes in secondary schools, *Support for Learning* , 9 (1), pp. 9–15.

Buzan, T. (1988) *Make the most of your mind*, Pan, London.

Campbell, R. (1985) *Developing the Primary School Curriculum*, Holt, Rinehart and Winston, London.

Canter, L. (1976) *Assertive Discipline: a Take Charge Approach for Today's Educator*, Lee Canter Associates, California.

Carpenter, B. and Bovair, K. (1990) Backlash. The Silly Season for Training, *British Journal of Special Education*, 17 (4), p. 136.

Carr, E. and Durand, V. (1985) Reducing Behaviour Problems Through Functional Communication Training, *Journal of Applied Behaviour Analysis*, 18 (2), pp. 111–26.

Carr, W. and Kemmis, S. (1986) *Becoming Critical: Education, Knowledge and Action Research*, Falmer Press, Lewes.

Chapman, N. (1994) Caught in the crossfire: the future of special schools, *British Journal of Special Education*, 21 (2), pp. 60–3.

Charlesworth, J. (1990) Don't be daunted by LMS!, *British Journal of Special Education*, 17 (2), pp. 53–5.

Clarke, J. and Wigley, K. (1988) *Humanities for All: Teaching Humanities in the Secondary School*, Cassell, London.

Clements, J. (1987) *Severe Learning Disability and Psychological Handicap*, Wiley, London.

Clunies-Ross, L. and Wimhurst, S. (1982) *The Right Balance: Provision for Slow Learners in Secondary Schools*, NFER-Nelson, Windsor.

CNAA (1991) *Review of Special Educational Needs in Initial and Inservice Teacher Education Courses*, CNAA, London.

Cooper, P. (1993) Learning from pupils' perspectives, *British Journal of Special Education*, 20 (4), pp. 129–33.

Copeland, I. (1994) The secondary school prospectus and the challenge of special educational needs, *Educational Studies*, 20 (2), pp. 237–50.

Corbett, J. (1994) It's his condition, mother: the medical model, in Sandow, S. (ed.) *Whose Special Need? Some Perceptions of Special Educational Needs*, Paul Chapman Publishing, London.

Coupe, J. and Goldbart, J. (1988) *Communication Before Speech*, Chapman and Hall, London.

Coupe, J., Barton, L., Barber, M., Collins, L., Levy, D. and Murphy, D. (1985) *The Affective Communication Assessment*, Manchester Education Committee, Manchester.

Davie, R. (1993) Listen to the child, *The Psychologist*, 6 (6), pp. 252–7.

Davies, B. (1994) On the neglect of pedagogy in educational studies and its consequences, *British Journal of In-service Education*, 20:1, pp. 17–36.

Department for Education (1992) *Initial Teacher Training (Secondary Phase)*, Circular 9/92, DfE, London.

Department for Education (1993) *The Education (Special Educational Needs) Regulations, No. 1047*, DfE, London.

Department for Education (1994) *Code of Practice on the Identification and Assessment of Special Educational Needs*, DfE, London.

Department for Education (1994) *Pupils with Problems*, Circulars 8–13, DfE, London.

Department for Education, *Reports on Pupils Achievements*, Circular 16/93.

Department of Education and Science (1970) *Education (Handicapped Children) Act*, HMSO, London.

Department of Education and Science (1975) *A Language for Life* (The Bullock Report), HMSO, London.

Department of Education and Science (1978) *The Education of Handicapped Children and Young People* (The Warnock Report), HMSO, London.

Department of Education and Science (1984) *Initial Training of Teachers: Approval of Courses*, DES, London.

Department of Education and Science (1989a) *The Education (School Curriculum and Related Information) Regulations 1981*, Circular 14/89, DES, London.

Department of Education and Science (1989b) *Discipline in Schools* (The Elton Report), HMSO, London.

Department of Education and Science (1990) *Special Educational Needs in Initial Teacher Training*, DES, London.

Diamond, C. (1993) A reconsideration of the role of SEN support services: Will they get in on the act?, *Support for Learning*, 8 (3), pp. 91–8.

Diniz, F. (1991) Special Education: an Overview of Recent Changes, *European Journal of Teacher Education*, 14 (2), pp. 107–15.

Donaldson, M. (1989) *Sense and Sensibility*, University of Reading, Reading.

Donaldson, M. and Reid, J. (1982) Language Skills and Reading: A Developmental Perspective, in Hendry, A. (ed.) *Teaching Reading: The Key Issues*, Heinemann, London.

Doyle, P. and Rickman, R. (1989) LMS: Implications for the 18 per cent, *British Journal of Special Education*, 16 (2), pp. 77–8.

Durand, V. M. (1990) *Severe Behaviour Problems*, Guildford Press, London.

Dyson, A. (1990) Special Educational Needs and the Concept of Change, *Oxford Review of Education*, 16 (1), pp. 53–66.

Dyson, A., Millward, A. and Skidmore, D. (1994) Beyond the Whole School Approach: an Emerging Model of Special Needs Provision in Secondary Schools, *British Educational Research Journal*, 20 (3), pp. 301–17.

Edwards, T. (1992) Change and reform in initial teacher education, *NCE Briefing No.9*, Paul Hamlyn Foundation, London.

Eisner, E. (1985) Instructional and expressive objectives, in Golby, M., Greenwald, J. and West, R. (eds.) *Curriculum Design*, Croom Helm, Beckenham.

Elliott, J. (1991) 'A model of professionalism and its implications for teacher education, *British Educational Research Journal*, 17 (4), pp. 309–18.

Emerson, E., Barrett, S., Bell, C., Cummins, R., McCool, C., Toogood, A. and Mansell (1987) *Developing Services for People with Severe Learning Difficulties and Challenging Behaviour*, Institute of Social and Applied Psychology, University of Kent.

Fagg, S., Aherne, P., Skelton, S. and Thornber, A. (1990) *Entitlement for All in Practice*, David Fulton, London.

Farrell, P. (1992) Behavioural teaching: a fact of life, *British Journal of Special Education*, 19 (4), pp. 145–8.

Fish, D., Twinn, S. and Purr, B. (1991) *Promoting Reflection: Improving the Supervision of Practice in Health Visiting and Initial Teacher Training*, West London Institute of Higher Education, Twickenham.

Florek, A. (1986) Backlash. Integration – or Bandwagon Hypocrisy?, *British Journal of Special Education*, 13 (2), p. 52.

Frude, N. and Gault, H. (eds.) (1984) *Disruptive Behaviour in Schools*, Wiley, Chichester.

Foxen, T. and McBrien, J. (1981) *Training Staff in Behavioural Methods*, Manchester University Press, Manchester.

Furlong, J. (1992) Reconstructing professionalism: ideological struggle in initial teacher education, in Arnot, M. and Barton, L. (eds.) *Voicing Concerns: Sociological Perspectives on Contemporary Education Reforms*, Triangle Books, Wallingford.

Gains, C. (1994) Editorial, *Support for Learning*, 9 (3), p. 102.

Gale, A. (1991) The school as organisation: new roles for psychologists in education, *Educational Psychology in Practice*, 7 (2), pp. 67–73.

Garner, P. (1994) Oh, my God, Help! What newly qualifying teachers think of special schools, in Sandow, S. (ed.) *Whose Special Need? Some Perceptions of Special Educational Needs*, Paul Chapman Publishing, London.

Garner, P. (1994a) *What Teachers Think about the Code of Practice*, Unpublished report, The West London Institute, Twickenham.

Garner, P. (1994b) Primary school prospectuses and special needs, *Education 3–13* (Autumn).

Garner, P. (1994c) Advocacy and the young person with special educational needs, *International Journal of Adolescence and Youth*, 5 (1/2).

Garner, P. (1995) Newly Qualifying Teachers and Special Needs, Paper to the International Special Education Congress, Birmingham, April.

Garner, P. and Sandow, S. (1995) *Advocacy, Self Advocacy and Special Needs*, David Fulton, London.

Gersch, I. and Gersch, B. (1995) Supporting advocacy and self advocacy, in Garner, P. and Sandow, S. (eds.) *Advocacy, Self-advocacy and Special Needs*, David Fulton, London.

Gersch, I. and Nolan, A. (1994) Exclusions: what the children think, *Educational Psychology in Practice*, 10 (1), pp. 35–45.

Gillham, W. (1990) *Basic Number Diagnostic Tests*, Hodder & Stoughton, Sevenoaks.

Goldbart, J. (1988) Communication for a purpose, in Coupe, J. and Goldbart, J. (1988) *Communication Before Speech*, Chapman and Hall, London.

Goldberg, P. (1989) *The Intuitive Edge*, Turnstone Press, Wellingborough.

Goodson, I. (1995) Ignore research at our peril, *Times Educational Supplement*, 31 April, p. viii.

Gore, L. and Mitchell, P. (1992) School-based training: a local education authority perspective, *Cambridge Journal of Education*, 22 (3), pp. 351–61.

Gregory, E. (1989) Issues of multiprofessional co-operation, in Evans, R. (ed.) *Special Educational Needs: Policy and Practice*, Blackwell Education, Oxford.

Gross, J. (1993) *Special Educational Needs in the Primary School*, Open University Press, Buckingham.

Gurney, R. (1976) *Language, Learning and Remedial Teaching*, Edward Arnold, London.

Handy, C. (1988) Cultural forces in schools, in Glatter, R., Preedy, M., Riches, C. and Masterson, M. *Understanding School Management*, Open University Press, Milton Keynes.

Hargreaves, A. (1990) Discourses of development. Unpublished notes presented to the JET International Colloquium, University of Birmingham, 1990.

Harris, J. (1987) Interactive styles for language facilitation, in Smith, B. *Interactive Approaches to the Education of Children with Severe Learning Difficulties*, Westhill College, Birmingham.

Harris, J. (1993) *Language Development in Schools for Children with Severe Learning Difficulties*, Croom Helm, Beckenham.

Harris, J. (1994) Language, communication and personal power: a developmental perspective, in Coupe O'Kane, J. and Smith, B. (eds.) *Taking Control*, David Fulton, London.

Hartley, D. (1991) Democracy, Capitalism and the Reform of Teacher Education, *Journal of Education for Teaching*, 17 (1), pp. 81–95.

Hewett, D. and Nind, M. (1987) Developing an interactive curriculum for pupils with severe and complex learning difficulties: a classroom process, in Smith, B. (ed.) *Interactive Approaches to the Education of Children with Severe Learning Difficulties*, Westhill College, Birmingham.

Hewett, D. and Nind, M. (1992) Returning to the Basics, in Booth, T., Swann, W., Masterton, M. and Potts, P. (eds.). *Curricula for Diversity in Education*, Open University Press, Milton Keynes.

Hill, D. (1994) Teacher education and training: a left critique, *Forum*, 36 (3), pp. 74–6.

Hinchcliffe, V. (1991) Two stages in the process of learning to read: implications for children with severe learning difficulties, in Smith, B. (ed.) *Interactive Approaches to Teaching the Core Subjects*, Lame Duck Publishing, Bristol.

Hinchcliffe, V. and SLD course team (1993) Review of NCC Curriculum Guidance 9, *Qwest*, 1 (2), pp. 18–19.

Hinchliffe, V. (1994) A special special need: self advocacy, curriculum and the needs of children with severe learning difficulties, in S. Sandow (ed.) *Whose Special Need?* Paul Chapman, London.

Holt, J. (1971) *The Underachieving School*, Penguin, London.

Houghton, J., Bronicki, B. and Guess, D. (1987) Opportunities to express preferences and make choices among students with severe disabilities in classroom settings, *JASH*, 12:1, pp. 18–27.

Humphreys, K. and Sturt, E. (1993) Challenging times for teachers, *British Journal of Special Education*, 20 (3), pp. 97–9.

Ireson, J. (1992) Collaboration in support systems, *British Journal of Special Education*, 19 (2), pp. 56–8.

Irwin, K. (1991) 'Teaching children with Down's Syndrome to add by counting on, *Education and Treatment of Children*, 14 (2).

Iwatta, B. A., Pace, G. M., Walsher, M. J., Cowdery, G. E. and Cataldo, M. F. (1990) Experimental Analysis and Extinction of Self Injurious Escape Behaviour, *Journal of Applied Behaviour Analysis*, 23 (1), pp. 11–27.

Jones, R. and Connell (1993) Ten Years of Gentle Teaching: Much ado About Nothing? *The Psychologist*, December.

Jones, R. and Miller, B. (1994) The Social Construction of Challenging Behaviour: Some Cautionary Notes, *British Journal of Special Education*, 21 (3), pp. 127–8.

Jordan, R. and Powell, S. (1990) *The Special Curricular Needs of Autistic Children: Learning and Thinking Skills*, The Association of Head Teachers of Autistic Children and Adults.

Kiernan, C. and Reid, B. (1987) *The Pre-verbal Communication Schedule (PVCS)*, NFER/Nelson, Windsor.

Knight, P. (1992) Secondary schools in their own words: the image in school prospectuses, *Cambridge Journal of Education*, 22, pp. 55–67.

Lacey, P. and Lomas, J. (1993) *Support Services and the Curriculum*, David Fulton, London.

Lawlor, S. (1990) *Teachers Mistaught: Training Theories or Education in Subjects?* Centre for Policy Studies, London.

Leeming, K., Swann, W., Coupe, J. and Mittler, P. (1979) *Teaching Language and Communication to the Mentally Handicapped*, Evans/Methuen Educational, London.

Lewis, A. (1991) *Primary Special Needs and the National Curriculum*, Routledge, London.

Lowenstein, I. F. (1970) A study of the needs of the schools' psychological service in one county, assumed by headteachers, *Bulletin of the British Psychological Society*, 23, pp. 37–9.

Lucas, D. (1989) Implications for educational psychology services of the Education Reform Act 1988, *Educational Psychology in Practice*, 5, pp. 171–8.

Luft, J. and Ingram, H. (1955) *The Johari Window: A Graphic Model for Interpersonal Relations*, University of California, Los Angeles, Extension Office.

Lunt, I. (1990) Local management of schools and education, in Daniels, H. and Ware, J. (eds.) *Special Educational Needs and the National Curriculum*, Kogan Page, London.

Lyon, C. (1944) *Legal Issues Arising from the Care, Control and Safety of Children with Learning Disabilities who also Present Severe Challenging Behaviour*, The Mental Health Foundation, London.

MacLure, M. (1989) Anyone for INSET? Needs identification and personal/professional development, in McBride, R. (ed.) *The In-service Training of Teachers*, Falmer Press, Lewes.

McBrien, J., Farrell, P. and Foxen, T. (1992) *EDY Trainee Workbook*, 2nd edition, Manchester University Press.

McConkey, R. and McEvoy, J. (1986) Games for learning to count, *British Journal of Special Education*, 13 (2).

McCulloch, M. (1993) What is involved in good school based teacher education?, *Journal of Teacher Development*, 2 (1), pp. 39–45.

McEvoy, J. (1989) From counting to arithmetic: the development of early number skills, *British Journal of Special Education*, 16 (3).

McGee, J., Menolascino, F. J., Hobbs, D. C. and Menousek, P. E. (1987) *Gentle Teaching: a Non-Aversive Approach to Helping Persons with Mental Retardation*, Human Sciences Press, New York.

McNamara, D. (1992) The reform of initial teacher education in England and Wales: teacher competence; panacea or rhetoric?', *Journal of Education for Teaching*, 18 (3), pp. 273–85.

Menolascino, F. J. and McGee, J. (1983) Persons with Severe Mental Retardation and Behavioural Challenges, *Journal of Psychiatric Treatment and Evaluation*, 5, pp. 187–93.

Miles, S., Barrett, E., Barton, L., Furlong, J., Galvin, C. and Whitty, G. (1993) Initial teacher education in England and Wales: a topography, *Research Papers in Education*, 8, pp. 275–305.

Mittler, P. (1992) Educational Entitlement in the Nineties, *Support for Learning*, 7 (4), pp. 145–51.

Mittler, P. (1993) Preparing all initial teacher training students to teach children with special educational needs: a case study from England, *European Journal of Special Needs Education*, 7, pp. 1–10.

Mongon, D. and Hart, S. (1989) *Improving Classroom Behaviour: New Direction for Teachers and Pupils*, Cassell, London.

Morant, R. (1981) *In-Service Education within the School*, Allen and Unwin, London.

Moses, D. (1982) Special educational needs: the relationship between teacher assessment, test scores and classroom behaviour, *British Educational Research Journal*, 8 (2), pp. 111–22.

Murphy, G. (1985) *Self Injurious Behaviour*, BIMH.

National Union of Teachers (1993) *Survey on LEA Centrally Held Special Needs Support Services*, NUT, London.

National Curriculum Council (1989) *A Curriculum for All*, NCC, York.

Nind, M. and Hewett, D. (1994a) Returning to the basics: a curriculum at Harperbury Hospital School, in Booth, T., Swann, W., Masterton, M. and Potts, P. (eds.) *Curricula for Diversity in Education*, OUP, Milton Keynes.

Nind, M. and Hewett, D. (1994b) *Access to Communication*, David Fulton, London.

Norwich, B. (1991) *Reappraising Special Needs Education*, Cassell, London.

OFSTED (1993) *Framework for the Inspection of Schools*, DfE, London.

OFSTED (1995) *New Framework for the Inspection of Schools*, DfE, London.

Ouvry, C. (1991) Access for pupils with profound and multiple learning difficulties, in

Ashdown, R., Carpenter, B. and Bovair, K. (eds.) *The Curriculum Challenge*, Falmer Press, London.

Palmer, C., Redfern, R. and Smith, K. (1994) The Four P's of Policy, *British Journal of Special Education*, **21** (1), pp. 4–6.

Peter, M. (1989) Local management and schools, *British Journal of Special Education*, 16 (2), pp. 75–6.

Pollard, A. and Tann, S. (1987) *Reflective Teaching and the Primary School*, Cassell, London.

Quicke, J. (1984) 'The role of the educational psychologists', in Barton, L. and Tomlinson, S. (eds.) *Special Education and Social Interests*, Croom Helm, Beckenham.

Reid, J. F. (1983) Into Print: Reading and Language Growth, in Donaldson, M., Grieve, R. and Pratt, C. (eds.) *Early Childhood Development and Education*, Guildford Press, London.

Roaf, C. (1989) Developing Whole School Policy: a Secondary School Perspective, in Roaf, C. and Bines, H. (eds.) *Needs, Rights and Opportunities: Developing Approaches to Special Education*, Falmer, Lewes.

Rogoff, B. and Wertsch, J. (1984) *Learning in the Zone of Proximal Development*, Jossey-Bass, London.

Russell, P. (1994) The Code of Practice : new partnerships for children with special educational needs, *British Journal of Special Education*, 21 (2), pp. 48–52.

Sacken, D. (1989) Due process and democracy; participation in school disciplinary processes, *Urban Education*, 23 (4), pp. 327–47.

Sandow, S. (1994) More ways than one: models of special needs, in Sandow, S. (ed.) *Whose Special Need? Some Perceptions of Special Educational Needs*, Paul Chapman Publishing, London.

Schaffer, H. (1977) *Studies in Mother-Infant Interaction*, Academic Press, New York.

Schon, D. (1983) *The Reflective Practitioner*, Basic Books, New York.

Schon, D. (1987) *Educating the Reflective Practitioner*, Jossey-Bass, San Francisco.

Schostak, J. (1983) *Maladjusted Schooling*, Falmer, Lewes.

Schwebel, M. and Raph (1974) *Piaget in the Classroom*, Routledge, London.

SEAC (1990) *A Guide to Teacher Assessment*, SEAC/Heinemann, London.

Shearer M. and Shearer, D. (1972) The Portage Project, a model for early childhood education, *Exceptional Children*, 38, pp. 210–17.

Simmons, K. (1994) Decoding a new message, *British Journal of Special Education*, 21 (2), pp. 56–9.

Smith, B. (1987) *Interactive Approaches to the Education of Children with Severe Learning Difficulties*, Westhill College, Birmingham.

Smith, B. (1988) Which approach: the education of children with severe learning difficulties, *Mental Handicap*, 17 (3), pp. 11–115.

Smith, B. (1991) *Interactive Approaches to Teaching the Core Subjects*, Lame Duck Publishing, Bristol.

Smith, F. (1978) *Understanding Reading*, Holt, Rinehart and Winston, New York.

Smith, F. (1986) *Reading*, Cambridge University Press, Cambridge.

Solity, J. and Raybould, E. (1988) *A Teacher's Guide to Special Needs, a Positive Response to the 1981 Education Act*, OUP, Milton Keynes.

Staff of Rectory Paddock School (1983) *In Search of a Curriculum*, Robin Wren Publications, Sidcup.

Stenhouse, L. (1975) *An Introduction to Curriculum Research and Development*, Heinemann, London.

Stern, D. (1977) *The First Relationship*, Harvard University Press, Cambridge.

Thomas, D. (1993) Gritty, sensible and utilitarian – the only model? Special educational needs initial teacher training and professional development, in Dyson, A. and Gains, C. (eds.) *Rethinking Special Needs in Mainstream Schools*, David Fulton, London.

Thomas, G. (1986) Integrating personnel in order to integrate children, *Support for Learning*, 1, 1, pp. 19–25.

Thomas, G. (1992) *Effective Classroom Teamwork: Support or Intrusion?* Routledge, London.

Thomas, G. and Feiler, A. (eds.) (1988) *Planning for Special Needs*, Blackwell, Oxford.

Tilstone, C. (1991) *Teaching Children with Severe Learning Difficulties*, David Fulton, London.

Tomlinson, S. (1982) *A Sociology of Special Education*, Routledge & Kegan Paul, London.

Trevarthan, C. (1977) Descriptive analyses of infant communicative behaviour, in Schaffer, H. (ed.) *Studies in Mother-Infant Interaction*, Academic Press, New York.

Visser, J. (1986) Support: a description of the work of the SEN professional, *Support for Learning*, 1:4, pp. 5–8.

Vlachou, A. and Barton, L. (1994) Inclusive Education: Teachers and the Changing Culture of Schooling, *British Journal of Special Education*, 21 (3), pp. 105–7.

Vygotsky, L. (1966) *Thought and Language*, MIT Press, Cambridge, Mass.

Whitaker, P. (1995) *Managing to Learn*, Cassell, London.

Wilson, M. (1985) *History for Children with Learning Difficulties*, Hodder and Stoughton, London.

Winchurst, C., Kroese, B. and Adams, J. (1992) Assertiveness training for people with a mental handicap, *Mental Handicap*, (20) 3, pp. 97–101.

Wolfendale, S. (1987) *Primary Schools and Special Needs: Policy, Planning and Provision*, Cassell, London.

Wolfendale, S. (1989) Parental involvement: Parental involvement and power-sharing in special needs, in Wolfendale, S. (ed.) *Parental Involvement: Developing Networks between School, Home and Community*, Cassell, London.

Wright, H. and Payne, T. (1979) *An evaluation of a School's Psychological Service – the Portsmouth Pattern in summary*, Hampshire Education Department, Basingstoke.

Zarowska, E. and Clements, J. (1988) *Problem Behaviour in People with Severe Learning Disabilities*, Croom Helm, London.

Index